Alternative Teaching Strategies
Helping Behaviorally Troubled Children Achieve

A Guide for Teachers and Psychologists

Marshall S. Swift, Ph.D. and George Spivack, Ph.D.

Hahnemann Community Mental Health / Mental Retardation Center
Department of Mental Health Sciences
Hahnemann Medical College and Hospital
Philadelphia, Pennsylvania

Research Press 2612 N. Mattis Avenue, Champaign, IL 61820

To our families

Naomi, Rod and Randy

Jane, Jason and Jonathan

Contents

FOREWORD   *xiii*

ACKNOWLEDGMENTS   *xix*

1   PROBLEM BEHAVIORS IN THE CLASSROOM   1

The extent of the problem   3

Specific behavior dimensions related to learning   6

2   INCREASING ATTENTIVENESS, DECREASING WITHDRAWAL   13

Alternative teaching strategies   14

Finding out the reasons why   15

Immediate attention-getting strategies   18

Decreasing work time   20

Increasing novelty, excitement and involvement   20

Bringing the student's thoughts
and interests into the learning process   21

Planning instructions   23

Responding to and rewarding attending behaviors   24

Sharing responsibility between student and teacher   26

Summary   27

3   *PROGRAMMING FOR THE OVERRELIANT,*
INTELLECTUALLY DEPENDENT STUDENT *31*

Alternative teaching strategies *33*

Getting the work started and keeping it going 34

Decreasing external reliance 37

Fostering and supporting internal direction and thinking 40

Maintaining independence 42

Summary *44*

4   *FOSTERING*
THE STUDENT-TEACHER RELATIONSHIP *47*

Alternative teaching strategies *48*

Learning about each other 50

Establishing fairness and consistency 52

Creating an atmosphere of positive feeling 53

Summary *57*

5   *SLOWING DOWN*
THE IMPATIENT, UNREFLECTIVE CHILD *61*

Alternative teaching strategies *63*

Maintaining attention to directions 63

Communicating the value of quality over speed 66

Focusing upon review 68

Educating reflectiveness 70

Encouraging planning 74

Summary *75*

6 INCREASING INITIATIVE AND INVOLVEMENT 79

Alternative teaching strategies 80
Relating school to the child's world 81
Expanding the child's view of himself in his world 84
Relating school to the child 85
Creating an atmosphere to encourage involvement 87
Encouraging the verbalization of ideas 91
Summary 93

7 PROMOTING RELEVANT TALK 95

Alternative teaching strategies 97
Clarifying social rules and external demands 98
Educating reflectiveness 101
Relating answers to questions 102
Distinguishing between reality and fantasy 106
Legitimizing fantasy 108
Summary 109

8 COPING WITH NEGATIVE FEELINGS AND ACTIONS 113

Alternative teaching strategies 116
Spelling out the rules and defining limits 117
Establishing personal contact 120
Overcoming crises 121
Airing dissent and questioning school 122
Providing alternatives 123
Providing structure and predictability 131

Dealing with accompanying emotions   133

Using outside resources   134

Summary   *135*

9   *ALLAYING ACHIEVEMENT ANXIETY*   *141*

Alternative teaching strategies   *145*

Private talks between teacher and student   146

Providing a reasonably pressure-free environment   147

Fostering self-esteem   149

Encouraging performance with tolerable anxiety   151

Summary   *154*

10   MEETING THE NEEDS OF THE
RESTLESS, SOCIALLY OVERINVOLVED STUDENT   *159*

Alternative teaching strategies   *161*

Legitimizing energy release   161

Clarifying and articulating the issues   165

Signaling   168

Selective use of attention   170

Reprimand and punishment   171

Using physical placement in the classroom   173

Capitalizing upon social motivation   174

Aiding the student to monitor his own behavior   178

Contracting   179

Summary   *180*

11 FOSTERING THE STUDENT'S VIEW THAT WHAT HE DOES MAKES A DIFFERENCE 185

Alternative teaching strategies 187

Checking the reality of the student's claims 187

Discussing the youngster's feelings
and linking his efforts to his work 190

Recording success 191

Emphasizing student initiatives 192

Summary 193

12 COMMON ELEMENTS IN TEACHING STRATEGIES 195

General considerations 196

Change takes time 196

What the teacher does makes a difference 197

The teacher as an initiator 197

Common elements of teaching strategies 198

One-to-one contact between teacher and child 198

The teacher as a model 201

The positive classroom environment 202

Clarifying environmental demands 204

Fostering self-control and independent problem-solving 206

The general and the specific 208

REFERENCES 209

Foreword

It is well within the role of the teacher and school psychologist to be skilled in identifying and communicating about children's classroom behaviors that are relevant to academic learning. Furthermore, teachers, teacher trainers and classroom consultants should have knowledge available to them about what to do to increase the effectiveness of each child's classroom behavior so that learning may be more efficient, pleasant, and probable, and the child a happier person.

A major step towards increasing classroom success would be the creation of a feasible and reliable method by which any teacher might identify which behaviors indicate effective and ineffective responses to the demands of the academic environment. Beyond allowing for better understanding of the child in the classroom, such an identification procedure could become the basis for the planning of specific alternative teaching strategies to help the child in trouble.

In order to aid in assessing and programming for children who display behaviors which impede learning, this book provides two major kinds of information: specific information about overt classroom behaviors that affect or reflect academic success or failure, and information and suggestions about alternative teaching strategies that may be used to increase behavioral effectiveness and subsequent academic achievement.

Until now there has not been a readily available nor widely recognized system for teachers to identify and to communicate to others about classroom behaviors proven to be related to learning. The focus of this book is on specific behaviors, behavior groupings, and total behavior patterns of children which, through a long series of research projects, have been shown to describe and distinguish successful and unsuccessful students throughout the elementary school grades. This focus is coupled with extensive step-by-step descriptions of alternative teaching strategies that can be practically incorporated into plans for each child or groups of children in the classroom. Such information is of concrete help to teachers and also provides the classroom consultant with a range of realistic recommendations that may be made to teachers and parents.

Almost ten years ago the authors began a long series of studies of the overt classroom behaviors of children, examined how these behaviors relate to each other and to academic achievement, and developed ways of measuring and profiling these behaviors which can be applied in the classroom. Out of this work it is now possible to identify both positive and negative behaviors that should be of concern because they reflect the child's response to the classroom and his subsequent ability to perform in a way that fosters learning. Following the identification of relevant classroom behaviors in urban and suburban schools and in regular and special classrooms in the United States, in traditional classrooms in France, and in open classrooms in England, we then approached the issue of alternative teaching strategies. To identify feasible alternatives, we worked closely with teachers in a wide range of traditional, special, and open school settings. We catalogued and discussed how teachers should handle these behaviors—how to encourage behaviors that enhance learning and redirect behaviors that interfere with learning. We then carefully combed the literature to discover what others have tested out by way of teacher reactions to and plans for these child behaviors. This book, then, has emerged out of these complementary approaches of *identifying academically relevant behaviors and what teachers should do about them.*

The information presented here is meant for teachers, psychologists, and counselors concerned about children in learning environments. It does not orient itself toward clinical symptoms of emotional disturbance, and is not meant as a diagnostic system for child pathology. While some of the behaviors described are symptomatic of emotional or social maladjustment (or adjustment, as the case may be), they are considered here because they have been shown to relate to classroom learning and not necessarily to psychiatric diagnosis. While the teacher is a needed co-professional with clinicians and parents when personal maladjustment of children is at issue, the teacher's main role must remain focused upon the child as a total *learning* individual. As such, his focus must be upon how well he enables the child to profit from the learning environment of the classroom, and his attention given mainly to those behaviors that indicate the child is profiting in that environment.

The content of this book draws heavily from research studies done by the authors, their own experience as teachers and parents, a total of twenty years working as psychologists and consultants in residential special schools and regular urban and suburban public schools, and highly focused discussions with experienced teachers in these settings. An attempt has been made to integrate all of these with what has been written by others interested in this broad field. While we rely heavily upon research, this is not a research report. Rather, our attempt is to place before teachers, parents, and consultants, in straightforward language, the results of our investigations, research and experience. At certain points the reader will be referred to published works he may read if he wishes to look more closely at a particular issue. An attempt has been made not to interrupt the flow of what is presented with references and examples of data that may mask or blur the main significance of the results for the reader who wishes to utilize the practical information provided. Our goal has been to present material in as useful and readable a fashion as possible.

In the attempt to present pragmatically useful information, theoretical discussions about child development and educational philosophy have been avoided. Certain biases, however, cannot be avoided in such a presentation, and a few words are warranted to make some of these explicit. The authors believe that the teacher plays *the* key role in the formal educational environment of the child in our culture. Furthermore,

> The teaching-learning situation can be highly therapeutic. It is fortunate that what is good teaching practice is usually also good mental health practice. In its concern for improvement of the child's academic performance, the school may thus not only help him to learn better, but may also improve his mental health.[1]

Alternative Teaching Strategies reflects this in directing itself to the teacher as the primary person in the formal educational life of the child. Experience suggests that sound educational materials, physical surroundings, parental involvement, psychological services, and administrative support all play an important role in the education of our children. However, the main funnel through which these operate is the classroom teacher who is in direct contact with children daily.

We feel that past attempts to help teachers appreciate the behavior patterns of school children have faltered from the inability or unwillingness of consultants and psychologists to appreciate the way children behave in the classroom and how this behavior relates to learning. On the one hand, there has too often been a clinical rather than educational focus, with suggestions as to what the teacher might do left vague or put in ambiguous terms. On the other hand, consultants concerned only with a theory of modification of specific behaviors too often do not concern themselves with identifying which behaviors relate to learning and thus warrant attention, nor have they demonstrated sufficient awareness that the pattern of a child's behaviors (both productive and nonproductive) describes his total response to the classroom atmosphere.

While our intention is to provide a new and practical system for use in classrooms, we have incorporated, where appropriate, material from a variety of psychoeducational and behavioral reports. Our focus is upon understanding and programming for children based upon the widest range of knowledge about classroom behavioral effectiveness as that behavior impedes or fosters learning.

The first chapter, concerning the proportion of children displaying disturbance in school, is presented to provide the teacher, and those with responsibility to help the teacher, with a realistic picture of how many children are having difficulty coping in the classroom. In part the chapter was prompted by a superintendent of schools who stated to one of the authors, "I was always led to believe that 10 to 15 percent of the children have problems in the classroom and based my planning on this belief. My suspicions are that that proportion is an underestimation. I need to know, so that I can work with my staff to plan accordingly, just what proportion of the children are displaying difficulty in our classrooms." We expand that quest in Chapter 1 to look at the proportion of children with serious classroom problems in urban and suburban communities in the United States as well as in a number of other countries. The reader will note that the superintendent guessed what many teachers already know: the problem is and has been far greater than his original figures suggested. In this chapter we conclude with the specific behaviors that identify a child's overall adaptation to and success in the *learning* environment. This information was gained in our many studies in schools in the United States, France and England. The end result of these studies is the ability to identify those behaviors in the classroom that reflect the student's effectiveness, use of his ability to learn, and the degree to which teaching alternatives are warranted.

Each of the next ten chapters provides extensive and detailed descriptions of specific, feasible teaching alternatives for working with students displaying each of the achievement-related behavior dimensions mentioned in Chapter 1. The approaches presented complete the descriptive-remediation (or preventive planning) loop wherein the teacher first observes and identifies a child's approach to activities and interpersonal interactions in the classroom, and then articulates alternative teaching strategies that may be used, based on the specific areas of behavior difficulty identified. The behavior dimensions described and for which detailed teaching alternatives are presented include:

inattentiveness and withdrawal from class activity

external reliance and intellectual dependence

rapport between student and teacher

impatient or unreflective behaviors

personal initiative and involvement in learning

irrelevant talk

negative feelings and actions

achievement anxiety

restless, disturbing behaviors

external blaming behavior

The focus of the last chapter is upon common elements among teaching strategies. Here we review previous discussions of alternative teaching strategies to point out basic, generally useful types of techniques which appear as common threads throughout the book. This understanding of general issues should provide further guidance in designing classroom environments to match the behavioral responses of students.

Footnotes

[1] T. A. Ringness. *Mental health in the schools.* New York: Random House, 1968, p. 24.

Acknowledgments

We are deeply indebted to a number of people who have supported and advised us in our work. This book would not have been possible without the enlightened support and encouragement of Dr. Clifford J. Bodarky, Director of the Hahnemann Community Mental Health/Mental Retardation Center. We view our work as part of a broad effort at early identification of disturbances in children, and the implementation of cooperative consultation and education efforts among schools and community mental health/mental retardation centers. The Center, under Dr. Bodarky's direction, has supported such an approach as part of the total mandate of service to those in need of quality care.

In accumulating knowledge and experience through the years, we have been assisted by more people than we could possibly identify by name. Major contributions have been made by teachers, psychologists and principals from the regular and special education programs of the School District of Philadelphia, especially those in the catchment area of the Hahnemann Community Mental Health/Mental Retardation Center, and staff of the Tredyffrin-Easttown School District, the West Chester School District, and The Devereux Foundation schools, all in suburban Philadelphia. Without the support, guidance and commitment of personnel from these schools, *Alternative Teaching Strategies* would not have been possible. Others providing information and assisting us in our research have included the faculties of elementary schools in Paris, France, the University of Paris (Laboratoire de Psychologie Génétique), and The Westwood Farm Country Junior "open class" School in Reading, England. Specific help during discussions of alternative teaching approaches was provided by teachers, counselors and principals from the Elwood, Miller, Potter-Thomas, Pratt-Arnold, Willard-Powers and Bishop Learning Center in Philadelphia, the St. Peters School of the Archdiocese of Philadelphia, the Berwyn Elementary School in Chester County, Pennsylvania, and the Bilingual Infant School in Waterloo, Ontario, Canada.

During the research phase of our study of teaching approaches, Linnea Back and Mitchell Kroungold made substantial contributions, as did Mimi Scheiber during the writing and editing phases of book preparation. Their research assistance and advice were highly valued.

1 Problem Behaviors in the Classroom

What proportion of children display behaviors that impede or reflect difficulty in learning or relating to others in the typical regular classroom? A youngster's classroom behavior reflects his success in participating in and benefiting from the educational enterprise. Many children display behaviors that detract from their learning progress. Some of them do so with sufficient frequency to give serious cause for concern. In fact, in almost every classroom there are children who have or will have significant behavioral difficulties during their school years.

At least 10 million of our young people under 25 . ˙. are crippled in their ability to learn, to relate to others, to see the real world as it is, or to adequately handle their impulses . . . they do not feel that they are a vital and effectual part of society. The future seems to promise only more such human tragedies . . . .

Research indicates that most children and adolescents with minor emotional and learning disturbances recover fully if they are given competent understanding, guidance and help. Most of the more seriously handicapped are found to improve with appropriate treatment . . . .

We must begin to apply tne knowledge we have toward active and vigorous programs of prevention . . . .[1]

As much as any other issue, teachers live with and talk about the problem behaviors of their students, at times in an attempt to better understand the students so as to better teach them; at times in an attempt to explain why a student is not achieving, e.g., "He doesn't pay attention to directions when I give them"; and at other times to justify referral to a school psychologist or counselor, e.g., "This child seems to have some deep problems."

Within the classroom itself, a large proportion of time may be spent attending to and planning for the problem behaviors of students. The focus of the teacher's attention, while most drawn to those with more intrusive problems, may also be drawn to the wide variety of students whose behaviors, though more benign, still may interfere with their academic progress. A 1972 national report sponsored by the United States Department of Health, Education and Welfare (USDHEW) revealed that in the typical regular classroom, teacher response to maladaptive behavior was "required frequently or occasionally for 66 percent of the boys and 42 percent of the girls."[2]

A first step in developing appropriate classroom approaches for such children is the realistic recognition of the extent of the problem. This knowledge is essential in the process of preparing the teacher for the "real world" of the classroom. It is the lack of appreciation of, as well as preparation to deal with, "non-academic" behavior problems which creates excessive stress upon the teacher. It is necessary, therefore, that we fully appreciate how many youngsters exhibit, even very early in their school lives, classroom behaviors that should cause concern. We must also recognize that without adequate identification and planning, these early behaviors often lead to alienation and academic failure as well as other emotional and social problems.

A second crucial step in the process of programming for the emotional, intellectual, and academic growth of children in school goes beyond awareness of the extent of the problem. It is also necessary for the teacher to know which specific behaviors affect learning in the classroom and therefore require careful attention and intervention, and which behaviors do not. Armed with knowledge of the proportion of children showing academically relevant difficulties in the classroom, the teacher is then ready for information and decision-making about what to do in the classroom.

The extent of the problem

Table 1 presents a picture of the extent of the problem over the entire age span, both in the United States and across national boundaries.* While the classification system is gross, the data clearly indicate that a large percentage of children have been identified by school or mental health authorities as displaying problematic behaviors. There is a remarkable consistency in these data, considering the fact that they were drawn from widely disparate geographic locations and at different times. Overall they suggest that in the average class of 25 to 30 students there could be three youngsters who are severely maladapting and between six and ten more whose behavioral adjustment is of sufficient concern to warrant some kind of special attention.

Beyond this general finding, some of the studies in Table 1 reveal other relevant information. Of those six to ten moderately disturbed children in the average class, as many have been found to be excessively inhibited and timid as have been found to be obstreperous, restless and defiant.[3,4,5] In other words, children have been identified as troubled not merely on the basis that they present a management problem to the teacher. Further, the presence of such problems as inattentiveness, restlessness and overinhibition have all been shown to relate to the youngsters' academic achievement.

---

* Where the studies use the term "moderate" or "unsettled" to describe maladjustment, these percentages are listed in Table 1 in the category Degree of Maladjustment: Moderate. Where severe difficulties were indicated, these are listed in that column in the table.

Table 1. Extent of maladjustment among children of school age*

Investigator/Reporter and Date	Place	N	Age or Grade	% of Maladjusted Students		
				Moderate		Severe
Wall, 1955	Eight Countries	–	Ages 5-16	22-42		4-12
Wall, 1956	Denmark	–	School Age		20-22†	
Chazan & Jackson, 1971	England & Wales	726	Ages 5-6		24†	
Pringle, 1966	England	9817	Age 7	23		13
Glavin & Quay, 1969	Rural Tennessee	–	–			13
Stennett, 1966	Rural Minnesota	333	Grades 4-6		22†	
Ullman, 1957	Rural & suburban Maryland	810	Grade 9	22		8
Bower, 1960	California	5500	School Age			10
Rogers, 1942	Columbus, Ohio	1524	Grades 1-6	36		12
USDHEW, 1972	United States	7119	Ages 6-11		17-22†	
Kellam & Schiff, 1967	Chicago, Illinois	2010	Grade 1		25-40†	
Silver & Hagen, 1972	Manhattan, New York	168	Grade 1	30		
Swift & Spivack, 1971	W. Chester, Pennsylvania	809	Grades K-6		40†	10
Swift, Spivack, Danset, Danset-Léger & Winnykamen, 1972	Paris, France	1325	Grades K-4		40†	

* See page 209 for complete references to these studies.
† Moderate and severe combined.

While these problems are more apt to occur among children of below average intellectual ability, each occurs among those of average or above average ability as well.[6]

Another and somewhat depressing finding is that matters seem to get worse as time in school progresses. A significant number of these behaviorally troubled children are not likely to resolve their problems without help, and will fall progressively farther behind in achievement.[7] The USDHEW report indicated that between the ages of six and eleven there is an increasing frequency of adjustment problems in the school. Our own data, from an ongoing longitudinal study of 500 urban children, have indicated that while one-third of the children when in kindergarten revealed some kind of behavioral difficulty, by third grade patterns of achievement-impeding behavior typified one-half of our group.

Investigations also have found that at all socioeconomic levels there is a surprising proportion of children who display moderate to severe difficulties coping with classroom and academic demands. A study of school children from deprived, working class and middle class backgrounds in England and Wales reported that one child in eight from a middle class home environment was displaying identifiable maladjustment in the classroom. Furthermore, there was a progressive increase in incidence of both severe and moderate maladjustment as one moved from the middle class to working class and deprived groups.[8] Studies of rural (e.g., Stennett, 1966) and suburban U.S. schools (e.g., Ullman, 1957) in Table 1 reveal that 20 to 30 percent of the children were identified as troubled. In urban classrooms serving disadvantaged communities as many as 40 percent of the children have been found to manifest some problem adapting to classroom demands (e.g., Kellam and Schiff, 1967). As already noted, our own longitudinal study of urban children has revealed that by third grade one-half of the children manifest one or another pattern of behaviors signifying serious problems in adapting to classroom demands. It is no wonder that as much as 80 percent of a teacher's day in a deprived area may be spent in trying to keep order,[9,10] and that teachers may have to interrupt classroom activities on the average once every two and one-half minutes in order to attempt some corrective action.[11]

Specific behavior dimensions related to learning

Once aware of the extent of the problem confronting us, it is necessary to examine more closely the nature of these behavioral difficulties. It is one thing to know that in an average classroom a number of children will have problems, and quite another to be able to identify which specific behavioral difficulties should concern us and become the focus of remedial effort.

The authors have carried out a number of studies over the past ten years in an effort to identify the specific classroom behaviors that indicate a youngster is having difficulty adapting, and to suggest why the difficulty occurs so that the teacher can take steps to alleviate it. Many of the studies are still in process; citations to completed work are provided in the Reference Section at the end of this book.

By way of summary, we initially collected a large sample of classroom behaviors judged as possibly abetting or interfering with learning. These emerged out of meetings with teachers from a variety of settings, a thorough search of the literature in the field, and our own experience working with teachers and students in normal and special class settings. Based on these experiences, we created rating scales that teachers could use. A large sample of elementary-age children were then rated, and with the use of a computer, it was possible to relate each behavior to age and sex of child, measured intelligence, actual academic achievement, and in some cases psychiatric diagnosis. It was also possible to group specific behaviors which tend to occur together in the same child so that instead of a large number of discrete behaviors we could now describe and talk about a manageable number of *behavior dimensions.* The dimensions retained for further study all related to achievement, independent of any relationship to IQ.[12]

To further validate these dimensions of behavior, each was related to a variety of background variables as well as achievement in another sample of children. This study confirmed the validity and significance of these behavior dimensions for learning, as well as the fact that the behavior dimensions do not change radically over short periods of time.[13] A subsequent study selected groups of fifth-grade academic achievers and underachievers, and demonstrated how these two groups differed significantly in the likelihood they would exhibit aberrance on these behavior dimensions.[14]

Since then, other studies have demonstrated that these specific behavior dimensions have cross-cultural significance for learning,[15] and how they relate to learning efficiency in an open-classroom setting.[16] In all of these studies, findings have been consistent in indicating that the greater the number of specific behavior dimensions in which a youngster is aberrant, the greater the likelihood he will fail or underachieve in school, and that there are certain patterns of aberrance that are particularly damaging.

The specific behaviors that comprise each of the ten dimensions are individually described in subsequent chapters. The dimensions are listed in Table 2 in order to present incidence of aberrance for each in both an urban disadvantaged sample of children and a "normative" group. The latter was selected as a normative group from a small city because the school district represented neither middle-class suburbia nor urban ghetto alone, but a cross section of family style and socioeconomic groups. Ten percent of this normative school population was black, and the measured IQ of the average child was close to 100. The data in the table are consistent with the more general data described earlier in this chapter, indicating that (1) in both groups, a significant proportion of children are displaying problems, (2) these problems are of greater dimension in disadvantaged urban than non-urban set-

Table 2. Percent of children aberrant on each behavior dimension in both the normative and urban samples

	Grade Level							
	Kindergarten		Grade 1		Grade 2		Grade 3	
	Norm N=101	Urban N=551	Norm N=121	Urban N=428	Norm N=118	Urban N=474	Norm N=107	Urban N=509
Inattentiveness and withdrawal from class activity	14	24	17	32	9	32	17	38
External reliance and intellectual dependence	14	23	17	36	9	35	20	40
Poor rapport with teacher	13	15	21	18	23	19	25	24
Impatient or unreflective	13	21	12	34	12	34	14	40
Lack of personal initiative and involvement	14	25	28	38	27	40	20	40
Irrelevant talk	19	24	17	29	9	30	18	30
Negative feelings and actions	12	20	11	35	8	35	21	43
Achievement anxiety	–	18	24	18	12	19	12	23
Restless, disturbing	16	17	13	32	12	32	23	37
External blaming	13	14	10	24	9	25	25	34

tings, and (3) there is a progressive increase in frequency of problem behaviors in all settings.

Summarizing, it is clear that significant behavioral difficulties in the classroom are typical of many children, in all settings. Not only has this been demonstrated through the use of gross classification systems, but also through the careful measurement of specific behaviors. We can now specify some of these behaviors and how they group together into problem dimensions.

The table and background studies also indicate that the behaviors comprising each dimension may be reliably observed by the teacher in the normal process of teaching, and that awareness of these behavior dimensions should add significant knowledge in deciding what ought to be done.

But is there reason to believe that the teacher can actually do anything about the behavior problems that emerge in the classroom? We believe there is, and this book derives from evidence that a teacher's understanding of where a child stands on each behavior dimension helps the teacher plan for that child. There is growing evidence to support the belief that the teacher plays a significant role in determining what occurs in the classroom and can alter specific problem behaviors, although they may be severe in some instances. [17] Our contention is that a major focus of teacher training and consultation to teachers should be on procedures that may be used in the classroom to identify behaviors important for learning and on what may realistically be done about them. The teacher is the one person who can observe children in a variety of specific learning situations over a period of time, and carry out a plan of action with a child as part of the "normal" school day. What the teacher needs, and has a right to expect from those who would help him, is specific teaching suggestions drawn from existing knowledge of specific problem behavior dimensions. This book outlines each behavior dimension, describes the behaviors comprising it, provides an interpretation of its meaning, and recommends alternative teaching strategies that can aid in the alleviation of the problem behaviors and can enhance the total educational environment.

Footnotes

[1] Joint Commission on Mental Health of Children, Inc. *Digest of Crisis in Child Mental Health: Challenge for the 1970's.* Washington, D.C.: Joint Commission on Mental Health of Children, Inc., 1969, p. 28.

[2] United States Department of Health, Education and Welfare, Public Health Service. *Behavior patterns of children in school. Vital Health Statistics* (J. Roberts and J. Baird, Jr.), 1972, p. 6.

[3] M. Chazan and S. Jackson. Behavior problems in the infant school. *Journal of Child Psychology and Psychiatry*, 1971, *12*, 191-210.

[4] United States Department of Health, Education and Welfare, Public Health Service, p. 37.

[5] S. G. Kellam and S. K. Schiff. Adaptation and mental illness in the first grade classrooms of an urban community. *Psychiatric Research Report 21, American Psychiatric Association*, 1967, 79-91.

[6] United States Department of Health, Education and Welfare, Public Health Service, pp. 45-53.

[7] R. G. Stennett. Emotional handicap in the elementary years: Phase or disease? *American Journal of Orthopsychiatry*, 1966, *36*, 444-449.

[8] Chazan and Jackson.

[9] M. Deutsch. Minority group and class status as related to social and personality factors in scholastic achievement. *Society for Applied Anthropology*, 1960, Monograph 2.

[10] J. W. Greenberg, J. M. Gerver, J. Challe and H. H. Davidson. Attitudes of children from a deprived environment toward achievement related concepts. *Journal of Educational Psychology*, 1965, *59*, 57-61.

[11] R. Dreikurs, D. B. Grunwald and F. C. Pepper. *Maintaining sanity in the classroom.* New York: Harper and Row, 1971, p. 187.

[12] G. Spivack and M. S. Swift. The Devereux Elementary School

Behavior Rating Scale: A study of the nature and organization of achievement related disturbed classroom behavior. *Journal of Special Education*, 1966, *1*, 71-91.

[13] M. S. Swift and G. Spivack. The assessment of achievement related classroom behavior. *Journal of Special Education*, 1968, *2*, 137-153.

[14] M. S. Swift and G. Spivack. Clarifying the relationship between academic success and overt classroom behavior. *Exceptional Children*, 1969, *36*, 99-104.

[15] M. S. Swift, G. Spivack, A. Danset, J. Danset-Léger and F. Winnykamen. Classroom behavior and academic success of French and American elementary schoolchildren. *International Review of Applied Psychology*, 1972, 1, *21*, 1-11.

[16] G. Spivack and M. S. Swift. Behavioral adjustment in the open classroom. *International Journal of Applied Psychology*, in press.

[17] M. S. Swift and G. Spivack. Therapeutic teaching: A review of teaching methods for behaviorally troubled children. *Journal of Special Education*, 1974, in press.

2 Increasing Attentiveness, Decreasing Withdrawal

Attending, concentrating and remaining alert are basic requirements for acquiring knowledge, or for responding appropriately to a task or another person. This dimension includes behaviors that indicate the degree to which the child pays attention to the teacher and orients his thinking and interaction around the content of classroom work. Teachers are rightfully sensitive about whether they have the child's attention when presenting material or giving directions. The relationship between attentiveness and achievement makes it crucial that the teacher be able to identify and program for children whose inattention reduces receptivity and decreases the time spent concentrating upon and responding to information or ideas important to learning.

Focusing attention is partially willful and selective and is a skill that slowly matures as the child grows. At all age levels, lack of attentiveness, irrespective of the reasons, is a clear signal of potential disruption of learning efficiency. The youngster with a short attention span, or a tendency toward quick shifts in attention, also has a tendency toward preoccupied thought which can cause extended distraction from important classroom activities. When the teacher is explaining something, he may notice that the child gets fidgety and looks away or that he has a faraway look in his eyes. Eye contact is difficult to establish and maintain and it is apparent that the child is oblivious to what is going on around him. The child may be difficult to reach because ideas or events unrelated to the immediate learning activities are occupying his mind. Without carefully planned intervention by the teacher, the attention of some youngsters will not be maintained.

The term "withdrawn" (with its social connotations) would almost suffice to describe these behaviors were it not for the specific cognitive characteristics also involved. Specifically, this dimension suggests the child's inability to contain or delimit the "pull" of inner thoughts for attention. Attention cannot be willfully directed toward important classroom activities and away from distractions. The child may not only be difficult to reach, but may forget what he has just said or lose his train of thought when he tries to respond. Sometimes the saliency of his inner thoughts reaches the point where he comes to class with one or two preoccupations, which he would talk about all day were he allowed. Among younger emotionally disturbed children this often occurs, as evidenced by the high correlation between these behaviors and the behaviors comprising the irrelevant verbal responsiveness dimension discussed in Chapter 7. These youngsters' responses are often irrelevant or poorly timed, and may reflect their own personal concerns.

Alternative Teaching Strategies

Most behaviors that militate against learning are active or outgoing, demanding some response from the teacher. The youngster does or says something in a manner or at a time which requires a reaction. In contrast, inattentiveness suggests an absence of behaviors important to learning. Thus it may easily be overlooked since it does not press the teacher for a reaction. As a result, appropriate responses may be less often spelled out and understood. In approaching this area of behavior, the teacher must consider three broad issues: the causes of inattentive and withdrawn behaviors; teaching techniques which can gain and maintain attention to academic matters; and teaching techniques which can make the inattentive youngster an active participant in the educational process.

Finding out the reasons why
It is useful for the teacher to inquire about the behavior of the inattentive, withdrawn youngster in other classrooms or academic settings. Is the behavior generally characteristic of him, or only true in certain academic content areas or teaching situations? How do settings in which he is inattentive differ from others, and what do the differences tell the teacher about what to change? Is he inattentive at places and times where he can be physically active (e.g., in gym); where free expression is encouraged (e.g., in art); or only in the more academic subject areas? A youngster may be inattentive and withdrawn when the situation is uncomfortable due to boredom (e.g., the work is too easy for him) or fear (e.g., the work is too difficult; the other children or the teacher frighten him).

In exploring possible causes, the teacher should talk with the youngster about his inattentiveness. It is dangerous for the teacher to assume too quickly that he knows what is driving the child away from attending to classroom matters. Patient listening may provide useful clues or at least a partial picture of the youngster's view.

Conversations can be started in a number of ways: "Sometimes we have things on our minds; can you tell me something about what you're thinking about?" "Sometimes things happen which are so important to us, it is hard to think of anything else; what are some important things that have happened to you?" If inattentiveness has been a recent occurrence, the teacher may discover that the youngster is concerned about something happening at home with his family. A quiet talk may lead the teacher to feel the parents should be included in a plan to alleviate the problems. A teacher may even discover that the youngster has not been aware that his mind has been wandering. Once the teacher understands some of the reasons, he can more effectively program to help the student refocus his attention on academic matters.

While working with one such youngster the teacher encouraged him to write down his thoughts whenever he realized that his mind was wandering, or whenever the teacher had to call his attention back to what was going on in the classroom. The teacher indicated that this would help him get to know the child, and it was agreed that the child would keep a notebook of "things that are on my mind." He was also encouraged to think of a good title for his "book." The child promptly entitled his book, "A Burden to My Parents and Teacher." The teacher then approached the situation in a manner which relieved this inferior feeling and fostered the child's belief that the teacher wanted to help him succeed in school.

Physical problems. There are many other reasons for inattentive behavior both within and outside the classroom. Outside influences, particularly in schools serving low income neighborhoods, may warrant checks into the youngster's general physical well-being, including his nourishment and whether or not he is getting enough sleep. In general, it is also good to check medical records for any indications of some physical basis for inattentiveness. The parents, as well as the school principal and physician, should be consulted. Inattentiveness is often one sign of lethargy and malaise due to hunger, fatigue or physical illness, as well as hearing and vision problems.

The teacher can also gain information by observing the child in various activities. Visual difficulties may be the problem for a youngster who displays an unusual amount of head moving while working at close range, rubs or blinks his eyes frequently, holds material too close to his face, tilts his head, frowns, scowls, or seems to be most inattentive when close desk work is required. Hearing difficulties may be a contributing factor to withdrawal from desk work when the student has frequent earaches, colds, or ringing in his ears; he may rub or pick his ears, tilt or turn his head in one direction, speak in a monotonous tone, or need repeated directions during listening activities. Whether these problems exist or not, but particuarly when they do, it is essential for the teacher to speak clearly and slowly, to be careful not to drop the endings of words, and not to attempt to speak over noise or to speak with his back turned.[1]

The classroom environment. In addition to a child's preoccupation with thoughts or any physical difficulties, inattentiveness may be due to the specific nature of the classroom environment itself. Thus, when exploring why a youngster may be inattentive or withdrawn, the teacher must not only be open to what the youngster directly and indirectly offers, but must also be open to designing specific alternative ways of reacting to this information. The teacher may have to go to great lengths in order to help an inattentive child. For example, one teacher reported that a youngster did well when alone, but became inattentive and difficult to reach in a group. While discussing this with him, the teacher found out that he was frightened of being with the group. During the discussion the teacher asked him where he would like to place his desk. The youngster said he would like to be in the coat closet. They finally agreed on a plan to place his desk near the closet and behind a file cabinet. He remained there each day for several weeks, attending well to his work as long as he was alone. No one was allowed to invade his "territory," but he was encouraged to come out if he wanted to. When he judged that the child was ready, the teacher assigned him to a task "you have to do," a task in which the youngster had to work with one other student. After the child accepted this, the teacher began to ease him into a variety of activities with that child, then with another child, and finally into small and then larger groups. As a further aid in reducing social withdrawal, the teacher also used role playing, with other children acting out situations in which a child was afraid of his peers: a new child's fear of others, a child's fear of larger children, and so forth. The youngster watched attentively, particularly when there was talk about how the make-believe youngster handled the troublesome social situation. The children were encouraged to tell about "what to do." The youngster agreed to have his desk moved back into the room after a short period of time.

If there is a specific situational cause, the teacher should work out a plan of action with the youngster. Remaining in contact with such a student is important, at times for no other reason than to intrude gently into his preoccupations and to let him know that others "outside" are interested in him. Saying hello in the halls, a private joke between teacher and youngster about it not being June yet, or a whispered comment such as, "I liked the way you were paying attention today," all help to create and maintain an interpersonal bridge. The youngster is then continuously reminded that he is not forgotten.

Beyond developing an interpersonal relationship, it is also necessary to develop a set of attention-fostering approaches and to plan responses for when the youngster is paying attention. Fostering attentiveness can be accomplished in a number of ways, centering particularly around care in giving instructions and directions, decreasing boredom and increasing excitement, bringing the child's thoughts and ideas into the learning process, and increasing his responsibility and involvement.

Immediate attention-getting strategies

While mainly of value for their immediate effects, certain strategies are necessary as part of any overall plan in working with inattentive and withdrawn youngsters. All of these strategies alert the youngster that he must attend to what is occurring or will soon occur in class.

There are a variety of techniques which communicate to students that the teacher is alert to their actions and that they are expected to be attentive as well. The teacher can pause after asking a question and look at different children before calling upon anyone to answer. Children can be called upon in a random rather than predictable sequence while the teacher alerts the entire class to the fact that anyone might be called upon to evaluate an answer given by someone else. He might say, "I am going to ask someone in the class to tell us what he thinks. I don't know who that will be yet so you have to listen to what is said so you can answer too." When a child is talking, the teacher should move around the room among the children, looking at them and encouraging them to look at the speaker. In this manner the teacher fosters attentiveness by alerting the children to the fact that they are accountable, and not out of the picture just because they are not immediately and directly involved at that moment.[2] Children can also be asked what they think will happen next or how a story will end. These techniques create a "level of uncertainty" which requires more than passive receptivity.[3] The degree to which the teacher varies his approach and provides challenge is closely related to the children's level of involvement during seat work.

The teacher can amplify these techniques by saying the youngster's name, or asking him a simple question when he sees that a child's attention is wandering. The child then knows that he should listen for something particularly important. His name may also be used to alert him to the fact that he will soon be asked a question or asked to respond to something happening in class. The teacher can also move closer to the youngster, put his hand on the youngster's shoulder, or point to something in his book or project while continuing to explain an idea to the class. At the start of the day, the teacher might talk with the child, and alert him to what he should listen for. The child can be told that he will be called on that morning to tell the class something about the subject being discussed.

Decreasing work time

One great cause of failure for the inattentive child is his inability to attend over long periods of time. Strategies that reduce the possibility of attention wandering during lengthy assignments, and that foster interest in what is going on by increasing the number of successful achievement experiences, will often help this child.

As a first technique, assignments should be designed to require only short periods of attention. Tasks should be delimited, shortened or broken into small parts. There are a number of ways to hold the child's interest in these shortened tasks. They may be separated by another activity or a brief relaxation period; they may be ordered so that the youngster must change his physical location or get up and move about. After each segment is completed, the teacher might require that the youngster show him the completed work, or discuss with him what was just read or done. The youngster then experiences the success of completion, or is quickly assisted when he goes off the track, which increases the probability that he will be able to finish the rest of the assignment successfully. These children very often do attend to tasks when they can succeed. The teacher may also consider adding variety by altering teaching methods, materials and content, although for the child with severe difficulties in attending, this should be kept to a minimum.

Longer work sessions may be introduced gradually. The teacher can have the youngster compete against his own best effort (i.e., the longest time working without losing attention) as a way to increase the length of time he can concentrate. It should be remembered that if such a child is to be successful, everything . . . must have a successful beginning and end within the known limits of his attention span.[4]

Increasing novelty,
excitement and involvement

Attentiveness is further enhanced by novelty, anticipation or a special task. The teacher can let the youngster in on the "secret" that a fun film is coming, or a special recess, gym or art period. The student may be asked to repeat directions to the class, or to read them from the board to the class. A special and attractive assignment may involve him. All youngsters like to operate audiovisual equipment. He may be asked to make his own flash cards, or to hold up materials the class is working from. And he may be asked to call on children at certain points during a lesson. Some materials have greater intrinsic interest than others, such as flannelboards, records, or other equipment that can be physically manipulated. Attention is generally held better when children are involved in manipulating learning materials rather than words or abstract symbols.

If students are to work together as a group, attention can be enhanced by decreasing the size of the group so that each child must become involved. Some teachers find it necessary to work on a one-to-one basis with the inattentive youngster, at least initially, slowly moving him into a group setting. Having him work with only one other youngster may help. Once in a group, the youngster should be placed with those he likes and who are themselves attentive and involved. Peers often successfully demand attentive involvement where the teacher may fail. Not only does the small group setting maintain a higher demand for attention, but the teacher is in a better position to find out what it is that interests the youngster and to use this later to hold his attention by relating it to academic material.

Bringing the student's thoughts
and interests into the learning process

Relating children's interests and ideas to classroom activities is probably a useful procedure for all children. However, for inattentive youngsters such an interplay of interest and classwork is paramount for decreasing the distraction caused by preoccupation with thoughts, ideas, interests or activities which pull their attention away from the classroom. The most useful strategies in the long run are those which allow an integration or fusion of what the youngster is thinking about or interested in and the academic material. The separation of classwork and what the youngster is doing is thereby reduced. By involving the child's interest, the teacher increases both the child's attention and his feeling of control over what is happening to him.[5]

The teacher can discover the child's interests by watching him carefully as he moves from one task to another. The youngster may be able to verbalize about what it is that captures his attention and, if not, others (parents, other teachers) may supply useful information. The goal is to reach and teach him as much as possible through those things which excite him. The teacher should allow the child to use his interests in class by giving a report or doing tasks related to them. If this is not feasible, his interests should be related to a specific subject area. For example, a youngster who loves horses may be asked to draw and label all the parts of a horse, thereby learning physiology and anatomy. He may be asked to report on how horses have been used through history: their role in battles, their significance to the Indians in the Old West, or to the knights during the Middle Ages. A youngster whose own preoccupations have led him into a special hobby or collection may be invited to present it to the class. The teacher must convey genuine interest in the child's concerns and preoccupations so that he feels that his private thoughts are valued and not dismissed or minimized; his thoughts must not be allowed to remain external to learning and a constant potential intruder upon attention.

To convey this respect for a youngster's private thoughts, it is important to guide him into classroom discussions with others, even if only in a small group. When appropriate, he can be asked to talk about a personal experience that pertains to the lesson. Whenever possible, he should be encouraged to verbalize his opinions. When attentively engaged, he may be asked to tell about what he is doing or has done. His verbalizing becomes a commitment of his own thoughts—his attention—to the learning process.

If the youngster daydreams, the teacher should avoid suggesting that daydreaming is unnatural or bad. He could say to the class: "Daydreaming is a necessary part of life. We all do it sometimes. This is how we learn to make plans about what we'll do in the future." The lights could then be turned off and the children told to put their heads down, and let their thoughts float around freely. "Think of flowers, or the rain falling; you're in a big bed, about to dream. Just let yourself think of anything that pleases you." After this the children could write down their thoughts or share them with the class.

The teacher's success at structuring a youngster's educational environment to take advantage of his inner thoughts and concerns depends in part on the educational philosophy of his school. The more "open" the philosophy, the easier it is to mesh the youngster's personal orientation with academic demands, since it brings the youngster into the planning of his daily tasks.[6,7] In most settings, however, teachers have some amount of flexibility in this regard, and this flexibility must be used to its utmost in order to encourage the inattentive, withdrawn youngster to emerge.

Planning instructions

Instructions provide a crucial point at which these children's attention can be caught or lost for the rest of an assignment. The risk of inattentiveness is greater when instructions are being given than when these children are actually doing their work. In spite of the importance and frequent use of instructions, most teachers are not aware that the way they are given has a great impact on children's ability to work successfully. While some children can handle a variety of different directions, the inattentive child will become confused and disorganized if told, for instance, to "write neater" one day, to "be more imaginative" the next, and then to "be careful of your punctuation."[8]

Verbal instructions should be short and free of excess verbiage; the essential information should be given simply, slowly and clearly. Teachers should also be careful not to habitually repeat instructions because the students may then only listen to the final statements. In effect, they are learning not to listen.[9]

Responding to and
rewarding attending behaviors

The use of rewards, praise and teacher attention are the most frequently discussed of all teaching strategies. A few specific refinements are worth adding when considering the inattentive youngster. As in all cases, it is better to reward the behavior you wish to see than punish what you dislike. Punishments for not paying attention by refusing to give directions again, or by telling the child that "If you didn't listen the first time, then you will have to suffer the consequences," do not help to increase attentiveness. Nor should the teacher ignore inattentiveness, assuming it will simply go away. The teacher must plan a positive strategy to reach the inattentive youngster.

When a total behavior that is desirable does not occur, it is necessary to reward behavior that approximates it or indicates an initial attempt at it. Even though a youngster may have remained attentive for only a brief period of time, it is a step in the desired direction. It must be noted and responded to: "I saw how you were watching Alan when he was explaining his chart. That was very fine." Whenever an inattentive youngster is attending, it helps to talk to him privately, not only to praise him but to discern what might have brought about or supported his attending behavior, and to articulate this with him. Such knowledge may subsequently help the teacher improve the youngster's learning environment.

The teacher's use of a simple but clear response can improve a child's attention and performance. For example, a child may be told "That's good" and tapped on the shoulder each time he spends a few moments attending to classwork. This simple approach has been used successfully with children who were very nonproductive and inattentive. One third-grade girl, for example, improved her attention and performance after a brief period of time, and a sampling of her papers showed an improvement in grades from F to C.[10]

Special mechanical devices. Since learning cannot occur if the teacher has no means for gaining and holding attention, it is imperative that he be able to provide an immediate, positive response to even a relatively brief act of attentiveness. If necessary, mechanical devices are available which can aid the teacher in increasing attentive behaviors which he can reward. The increased attentiveness can then be further rewarded with some tangible object or prized activity.

One of these mechanical aids is a box containing a light which can be flashed by the teacher. A box is placed on each child's desk and the class is told that each time they are paying attention, the light will go on. At the end of class, the children could be given candy or allowed to watch a movie. This procedure can also be adapted for only two or three children, thus decreasing the need for the teacher to get the child's attention. It also alerts the teacher, in a very direct way, to these inattentive children who may become lost to the teacher in the course of his efforts to respond to more active, disturbing behaviors.[11]

This approach can also be used without the mechanical device. The child's name can be written on the blackboard and a mark placed beside it each time a desired behavior occurs. This will call attention to the desired behaviors each time they occur and the teacher can then respond with a reward.

A second mechanical device used to increase the attention of a group of children is a hand-held, inexpensive and easy-to-use transmitter which the teacher carries as he moves about the room among the children. The transmitter is wired to operate a red light and a large wall clock. When all the children are attending, the teacher activates the clock by pushing the transmitter button. When a child is not attending, the button is pushed to stop the clock and to turn on the red light. The class can be told that in order to earn a special activity, they must maintain attention for a specified period of time; for example, 30 minutes during a one-hour period.[12]

*Sharing responsibility
between student and teacher*

The teaching approaches discussed above require that the teacher directly intervene with the inattentive youngster so that he maintains contact with classroom activities. Although the child may be unable to remain involved and alert without external assistance, the ultimate goal is for the child to take action for himself, without external intervention. When the child is personally and actively involved, particularly when he can experience success, he will become more attentive.

Another approach, then, is to increase the child's involvement and responsibility for maintaining attention by providing him a means whereby his own efforts lead to success. One such method allows the child to record his own attentive or inattentive behavior. The teacher defines for him the behaviors which indicate that he is paying attention: when he is looking at the teacher, doing an assignment appropriately and is alert to recite when called on. The child is then given an "attention recording" sheet printed with small boxes and instructed to place a "+" in a box each time he realizes that he is paying attention; to place a "-" in a box each time he realizes that his mind is wandering or he has been distracted. After a period of time, the child may be able to maintain attention without the self-recording procedure.[13]

A second method designed to increase the child's attention to a work task is having him record the time taken to complete the task. The aim is to alert him to a beginning and end point in time by recording each on the top and bottom of his work sheet. If the tasks are held constant, the child's attention can be focused upon completing the same number of problems correctly in less time. Children who can tell time can use a wall clock. For younger children, two clock faces

26

without hands can be stamped on their papers. They can then draw in the hands of the clock for start and finish times. This procedure has been found to be particularly effective with elementary level, emotionally disturbed children whose inattentiveness is a serious problem.[14]

Summary

Maintaining attention is crucial in the learning process. Planning for and with students requires that the teacher be alert to the fact that inattention constitutes a serious problem, even though it may not cause classroom disruption or upset others. The teacher can turn to a variety of information sources to aid in understanding the reasons for inattention and withdrawal. Discussions with previous and special area teachers can clarify whether the difficulty is longstanding or recent, and whether the inattentive behavior is pervasive or is appearing only in one classroom.

Careful observation of children whose attention wanders may reveal some difficulties requiring referral to resources outside of the classroom. To understand the problem more fully before taking action, discussions with the child are useful. This means that the teacher must remain open to the child's thoughts and actions and view them as guides to a plan for working together.

These youngsters are unable to maintain attention without some external assistance. External intervention may be built into a teaching plan in the form of immediate attention-getting procedures. The inattentive child need not be singled out even though these approaches are designed particularly with him in mind; instead the entire group may be alerted during a group activity.

The inattentive child will become more involved in class when he is provided with experiences leading to success. Since tasks requiring long periods of attention will only lead to failure, work for him should be assigned in segments he can accomplish, with the amount of time spent gradually increased. It is also helpful to plan work which creates a reason for the child to pay attention through novelty, excitement and the use of the child's own interests. While all the approaches mentioned may be effectively combined in a plan for one child, a good initial approach would include group-alerting techniques, brief and clear instructions, short tasks and interest-capturing materials.

To foster the growth of attentiveness the teacher must also actively look for instances, no matter how small, in which the child is alert, and capitalize upon these with a favorable response. Especially when the child displays other, more disruptive behaviors in addition to inattention, it is useful for the teacher to communicate recognition of attentive behavior with a tangible reward.

The ultimate goal is attention without intervention. Teaching approaches which allow for the sharing of responsibility with the student for holding attention on his own will move him a step further toward the attainment of the alertness and concentration needed for academic success.

Footnotes

[1] M. C. Austin, C. L. Bush and M. H. Huebner. *Reading evaluation.* New York: Ronald Press Company, 1961, pp. 59-64.

[2] J. S. Kounin. An analysis of teachers' managerial techniques. *Psychology in the Schools,* 1967, *4,* 221-227. Also in J. S. Kounin and S. Obradovic. Managing emotionally disturbed children in regular classrooms: A replication and extension. *Journal of Special Education,* 1968, *2,* 129-136.

[3] J. S. Bruner. *Toward a theory of instruction.* Cambridge, Massachusetts: Harvard University Press, 1966, p. 43.

[4] W. M. Cruickshank, J. B. Junkala and J. L. Paul. *The preparation of*

teachers of brain-injured children. Syracuse: Syracuse University Press, 1968, pp. 159-160.

5 Bruner, pp. 114-120.

6 T. Borton. *Reach, touch and teach: Student concerns and process education.* New York: McGraw-Hill, 1970.

7 T. B. Gregory. *Encounters with teaching: A micro-teaching manual.* Englewood Cliffs, New Jersey: Prentice-Hall, 1972.

8 T. C. Lovitt and J. O. Smith. Effects of instructions on an individual's verbal behavior. *Exceptional Children,* 1972, *38,* 685-693.

9 Austin, p. 63.

10 R. V. Hall, P. Lund and P. Jackson. Effects of teacher attention on study behavior. *Journal of Applied Behavior Analysis,* 1968, *1,* 1-12.

11 H. C. Quay, J. S. Werry, M. McQueen and R. L. Sprague. Remediation of the conduct problem child in the special class setting. *Exceptional Children,* 1966, *32,* 509-515.

12 J. Willis and J. Crowder. A portable device for group modification of classroom attending behavior. *Journal of Applied Behavior Analysis,* 1972, *5,* 199-202.

13 M. Broden, R. V. Hall and B. Mitts. The effect of self-recording on the classroom behavior of two eighth-grade students. *Journal of Applied Behavior Analysis,* 1971, *4,* 191-199.

14 R. Kroth. Behavior management techniques. Paper presented at the Council for Exceptional Children, 46th International Conference, March 1968.

3 Programming for the Over-reliant, Intellectually Dependent Student

All behaviors in this dimension indicate reliance upon others to provide guidance when confronted with academic work. For example, the child may need the teacher's specific directions on how to approach and proceed with a task. If the directions are not precise, he misses the point and becomes lost, needing to be told again how to proceed. The teacher becomes crucial not merely as an information source, but also as a guide for each step in the learning process. The child wants to do little, if any, decision-making and consequently the teacher is tempted to accuse the child of wanting him to do all the work.

Or, the child may rely on his peers for direction. He looks at other students even after receiving direction from the teacher, hoping to see what they are doing before attempting the task himself. Such behavior is frequently viewed in a moral context as cheating, but it is more significant as an aspect of his external reliance. He does not trust his own judgment and therefore looks to others for assurance because he views *them* as better judges of how to meet expectations.

In addition, the child has difficulty when he must make a decision by himself. Finally thrown back upon his own resources, he seems lost and unable to rely on his own judgment to figure out how to proceed. He may be slow to try something new or may give up when work becomes demanding or more difficult than usual. When matters become particularly stressful, his tendency to seek external guides is paralleled by a tendency to blame others for failure, and by a decrease in attentiveness to the teacher and academic activities. This attitude may become completely generalized: "Since you say what I will do and how, then it is your fault if things go wrong. And, since you have not made it easy for me to do this work, I won't do it until you solve the problem for me."

All of these behaviors have common elements. The youngster does not give direction to what he is doing. He cannot manifest intellectual initiative when it is required of him, or assume personal responsibility for what he finally does. The "powers" reside outside of him: they reside in the teacher, his peers, and what "authority" says. He is unable to assert himself through the learning process, and does not make decisions about what is important to him. He does not actively manipulate ideas or become involved in the learning process. As a consequence, he feels helpless and anxious when external supports and guidelines are taken away.

While this tendency toward external reliance is normal among very young children, the teacher must gradually replace it with "inner-directedness." The youngster who continues to be overreliant must gain a sense of himself, a feeling of self-confidence in his own judgments, and at times must also be allowed to resist external direction.

Overreliance is one of the more stable predictors of academic failure at every grade level and in both traditional and open classrooms. Without inner initiative, the student's ability to learn is greatly impeded. This is particularly true in the open classroom where independent functioning is closely related to the ability to understand what is happening in class, the application of what has been learned to new tasks, and knowledge of material when called upon in class. All of these behaviors reflect the child's comprehension of content and his ability to display that understanding. In the more traditional setting, a youngster may comprehend what is happening even though dependent upon external guidance about how to proceed since the teacher is more likely to tell him exactly what to do and how to do it. In the open classroom, comprehension of subject matter is more dependent upon the child's ability to function independently because of the greater demand for student decision-making. In both types of classrooms, but particularly in the open setting, this demand may be too much for certain children to handle, causing excessive anxiety in those who are reliant upon others for direction. Whatever the particular psychoeducational plan, the teacher must consider alternative strategies for youngsters who are unable to proceed on their own.

Alternative Teaching Strategies

Independence of mind and action does not come about easily and cannot be expected simply because adults assert that a youngster is "capable of doing his own work"; nor can a teacher ignore pleas for help by saying, "I explained the assignment and if you were listening carefully you would have gotten it." The overreliant youngster must be helped from intellectual dependence to self-reliance. It is important to recognize these behaviors as indicative of dependence in the learning situation, and to program for them as such. Labeling the child who is overreliant as lazy, "unwilling to try," or a cheater misses the underlying meaning of the behavior, frightens the youngster with rejection, and condemns him without helping him change his behavior. It may even create a situation in which dependence upon others increases rather than decreases, and some students may feel that the teacher will not help, and should therefore be rejected. Anger or other negative feelings and actions then further impede academic efforts and complicate the teacher's task. As reliance increases, problems are more likely to occur in other spheres of achievement-related behavior; for example, the youngster may become highly anxious, inattentive, or defiant.

The first and most crucial step in helping the overreliant student feel secure in the classroom is to enable him to approach learning tasks expecting a great deal of external support. The teacher must present himself as someone who can and will provide the necessary support and guidance for the child to experience success. Once the youngster feels he has such support, he will risk venturing out on his own. Learning tasks can be arranged with limited choices so that the child succeeds and recognizes himself as someone who can function without total support. Techniques involving less external guidance can then be introduced to foster independent behavior and thinking.

Getting the work started and keeping it going

Clarifying assignments. The child should initially be given assignments in a way which enables him to proceed. Inability to start working is a prime contributor to academic failure and increased behavioral difficulty. Quality and independent work are less important at this point than making it possible to start work and to follow it through. It may often be necessary to give precise directions so that relatively little initiative is demanded of the student. The teacher should not give last-minute, unexpected details and instructions that may be confusing and cause the child to wonder exactly what the teacher wants. After carefully organizing the directions beforehand, it is useful to present a task by saying, "I am going to give the directions about how to do this now. I want you to listen and repeat them." Then the child is given directions one step at a time. The teacher should realize that he may have to plan to present the instructions in a variety of ways so that the child is able to do the assignment. For instance, the child may benefit both from verbalizing instructions for himself, and writing them where he and the teacher can review them in the child's own handwriting. Even after he has written the instructions, the child will often need to rehearse them in a practice session with the teacher before actually proceeding on his own. In the practice session the student should be asked to read the first direction he has written, and then to begin at that point. When he has successfully completed one step the teacher can comment, "You've done the job. Now read step two and work on it." Once he understands how to follow instructions, in subsequent lessons a card with the steps outlined should be taped to the right-hand corner of his desk. This allows the student to check directions at any point, and allows the teacher merely to walk by, check the work, and point to a step not taken or to the next step.

For a young child or a non-reader, the steps can be presented on the blackboard in picture form; for example, a drawing of the youngster's workbook cover with a "+" sign on it and the page number. This would indicate to him that his first assignment is the addition problems on that page. A second drawing of an animal would indicate that feeding the pets is the second task, followed by a drawing of a faucet for washing the hands, a clock with five minutes marked to give the amount of time allotted, and so forth.

Assignments often must be broken down into several smaller lessons. Initially such youngsters must be told that there are a series of tasks to complete, but that there is a sequence and one task must be done first. The child then does not drown in choices since he does not have to make a choice. He acquires the expectation that the teacher will support him as he attempts the work. If he is unable to organize his work, he now knows that organization will be provided. If he gets lost, the teacher will get him back on the track by saying, "Let's go back and look at what we decided we would do today." The purpose of this is first to review with the child the work he has done successfully in order to foster confidence that he can do it. The teacher can then discuss with the child what might be done next and why. The teacher supports, and also provides a model of how to move through a task. As the youngster becomes successful at moving from one element in a task to another, work plans can be drawn for increasingly longer periods of time. Expectations can be stated: "How many of these problems do you think you can do this morning? I expect you to go right on by yourself in following the plan. If you have trouble, go back to the step before. Then if you need help, I'm here."

It is probably not useful to make a major issue of such a child's small decisions or his taking initiative by expressing an opinion. It might do no harm to say such things as: "I'm pleased you decided for yourself. You did make a choice. You can do it." But these attempts to encourage him may be counterproductive if they come too early because they are contrary to his view of himself and his belief in his abilities. The youngster who is overreliant sees himself as incapable of working on his own. To raise the issue of "who" he is relative to his work only draws attention to the fact that he sees himself as someone who generally cannot make decisions or carry out work on his own. This self-image changes slowly, and requires much patience and persistence on the teacher's part.

Using social approval. Even after the youngster has successfully started his work, he may need interpersonal motives to complete it. Very often these youngsters respond to the promise that they will be allowed to do things for or with the teacher if they sustain effort and complete their work.

However, for some youngsters the teacher's attention and support are not sufficient. The child's parents and peers can also be involved, as in the following case. A third-grade student, described as having "poor independent work skills," typically completed only a very small percentage of his arithmetic problems under the usual instructional approaches. He was told that if he completed 60 percent of his arithmetic work sheet, he would receive a note to take home to his parents to exchange for a surprise. His parents had agreed to this plan. The boy's initial work response was favorable but after the third day he returned to his previous non-productive level. The teacher then announced a new game in which the boy was to be class "engineer" if he started and completed his work sheet. The boy, as engineer, could earn his entire class a special activity if he completed his work and did not quit. Each day the class members were allowed to urge him on and to applaud him when he accomplished the goal. In this situation he achieved the goal almost 100 percent of the time. However, when "engineer" status was removed and the boy could not rely on the accompanying peer encouragement, support and approval, he once again returned to the poor level of independent work completion. He was too reliant upon others to work productively on his own. However, by varying the approach it was possible to increase his successful work completion, whether or not he was the engineer. This was done by allowing others to alternate with him in being the "engineer" who earned the special activity. A different engineer was selected after each class session. If the child who was selected finished his work during the next session, he received applause and was allowed to lead a special activity. The youngster in question was selected frequently but was no longer singled out as a special case.[1]

These approaches show that, though some teachers do not believe "cheerleading" can be effective in the classroom, these youngsters may actually respond best to genuine encouragement from those they respect. When the teacher's attention and support are not sufficient, then parents, and especially peers, can be powerful and productive forces which enable the child to complete his work successfully.

Decreasing external reliance

Independence is best fostered through a highly organized approach. The child should be taught to seek his own solutions and coached in the necessary behaviors. Teaching techiques must help the child see himself as capable of making choices, while not threatening him with the expectation that the "props" will be pulled out before he is ready to move on his own. The teacher can devise tasks and activities that require simple choices or small decisions which he knows the child is capable of making.

Teaching the child how to resolve problems. The emphasis here should be upon teaching the child *how* to think about his work so he learns that his attempts to make decisions are appropriate, and that his decisions should be based upon discriminating what is relevant to the problem. An example of such an approach with the dependent youngster is to ask him to state what he is going to do when confronted with a simple choice within a task or among tasks. "Are you going to do this, or this?" The teacher should then ask the child, "Which one are you not going to do?" The youngster should also be encouraged to discuss "what else" he will do and not do *after* he decides what he will do first. For the intellectually reliant child, learning to think to resolve problems is crucial if he is to master academic content.

Teaching the child how to evaluate choices. The youngster must also learn that he can evaluate his own choices rather than depend upon, or worry about, the teacher or his peers. Evaluative responses from the teacher such as, "That's good" or "That's not good" only maintain the child's belief that he needs external support. A less evaluative response can both successfully support the child's independent efforts, and at the same time teach him to think of what may result from his choice. The teacher can say, "That's one idea. What might happen next if you did that?" If the child falters and makes an effort to change his original idea, the teacher can indicate, "That's *another* idea. What might happen next?" Each choice can be written on the board and examined as "an idea." The child then sees that his ideas are valued, and that they can be examined to decide which one is best.

Teaching the concepts necessary for decision-making. To help a child become less dependent, the teacher should teach him how to handle problems himself by giving him an understanding of specific words and ideas necessary for decision-making: "I can do this *and* that, this *or* that, this and *not* that." Other concepts necessary to help the youngster think about proceeding on his own are the recognition of which things are the *same* or *different*: "Is this the same kind of problem as those we did yesterday? Are the problems different? If they are the same, how did you decide to do them before?" Or, if they are different, "How are they different?" To help the child decide what plan of action is best, the teacher must also introduce such concepts as "might" and "if": "If you do that, then what might happen?" This contrasts with the usual approach in which the child is told the consequences of his actions and not taught how to think ahead to evaluate a choice for himself.[2] Even in the earliest school years, the child can be taught to think of and evaluate his own ideas, thus increasing non-dependent, achievement-facilitating behaviors.

Using individualized instruction. It may still be necessary to have the child work on some task which is all his own so that he cannot look to others for help. It is better, however, to gradually steer him away from the individual directions which make him different from the rest of the class. Activities or tasks may be arranged so that each student must follow his own directions, or has a different set of directions. The teacher can review with him the reason for his decision, encourage him to articulate why he chose one thing rather than another, and discuss what outcomes he expected. It is crucial to avoid correction or the implication that there is a better way than the one he chose. Exploration serves only to bring the fact and process of decision-making into the open.

Working with peers. Some dependent children are more successful at earlier stages when they work with another child. This is particularly helpful when the more dependent child has some knowledge or skill that the other youngster does not have; he then does not have to depend on another person but can take the initiative. It is best not to place the youngster with a strong-willed, bossy peer. He may be easily overridden, or hesitate because his initiatives are overlooked or discouraged. A peer who can give and take is best. After a successful interaction in which the reliant child has shown he is able to contribute to, and carry out, work with a peer, he might be given the opportunity to tutor someone else in that area.

Fostering confidence. At this stage the youngster may "slip back," showing a need for external support and guidance. He is testing whether the teacher is still available if needed. The teacher must now emphasize his confidence in the youngster's ability to make choices and to rely upon his own judgment. The youngster may still desire to write out instructions, or wish to discuss them first with the teacher. These desires should be accepted without hesitation, but the child should be told that he is now able to make his own choices and that he should make every effort to try a task before asking the teacher or someone else: "You start it first, then I'll help you." "You do the whole page and then I'll talk with you about it. I want you to think it through first, as we did before." All activities should be presented with the expectation that the youngster will proceed by depending less upon the teacher. Thus, the youngster should receive continued encouragement to act independently within a fairly clear structure and set of expectations. The teacher should exert a gentle push for independence, yet support the youngster when he hesitates to make his own decisions.

Fostering and supporting
internal direction and thinking

From this point on teaching approaches must be aimed at enabling the child to see himself as independent. Independence may take the form of opposition: "That is not my choice. I do not want to do that. I want to do something else." Such assertion should not be challenged too abruptly, or viewed only as an expression of negative feeling. Although it is often tempting to deflate the youngster who exhibits opposition, particularly when he has no positive alternative to offer, it is better merely to ask if he has another thought. If he does not, the matter should be dropped without making a point of the fact that he has nothing to offer. The teacher should capitalize on this behavior as a display of independence, shifting from the earlier, highly organized approach to one which actively encourages the student to assert himself intellectually and to think independently. It is often useful to follow incidents of self-assertion with a class discussion about how a student might choose to do his work. The student can then be encouraged to tell about how he feels. He should be supported when he stands up for his own convictions (even if he overdoes it) because he must learn to define himself as different from others.

Allowing the student to make choices. If students are to gain confidence in their own ability, they must be allowed to take initiative and schedule their own work. The teacher can specify the work to be done for some part of the school day. The student is then allowed to do the work (e.g., math, spelling, etc.) in any sequence he chooses. If the work is completed before lunch, for example, the student is free to engage in any classroom activity until lunchtime. Thus, the student is first free to choose the order of his classroom work, and then able to use his judgment about how to use the free time he has earned by completing it. This approach might be used with increasing periods of time from half a day to a full day, and so forth.[3] Here it is appropriate for the teacher to let the child know that he did use his own judgment to decide what to do and how to do it.

Using different approaches to the same problem. Once the youngster realizes that he can have a different point of view and that he can make decisions on his own, materials which require different approaches to the same problem, rather than specific instructions, are useful: "How many different ways can you add up money to get 75 cents?" "What different ways can you go from your home to school, to a grocery store, to Peking?" The child can draw different maps to reach the same goal. He can be encouraged to describe "the different ways I can choose to go to the store." These exercises can be followed with discussions about how anyone decides how he is going to do something. In English and social studies the child can be directed to the use of editorial pages of the newspaper to point out that differences of opinion exist on any subject. He should be encouraged to develop his own opinion on the topic. Films and books can be used to show the different ways people live. Stories with alternative endings are also valuable; for example, "A boy was out camping and became lost in the woods. He had matches and a canteen of water." The student is asked to give different step-by-step alternative actions the boy could take to find his way out. Mystery stories may be read up to a point, and the group then asked to supply possible endings. A box or bag with something in it may be rattled, and each child asked to think of what it might contain, and the reasons why he thinks that. The question "Why?" is preferable to questions which can be answered by yes or no.

At this point the student will be less swayed by the opinions of others and less reliant upon them. He will feel he has accomplished something when he has successfully reached his own decision. The teacher should continue to communicate that the youngster, like everyone else, is entitled to his own ideas.

Maintaining independence

Even when all is going well, the teacher should remember that the overreliant youngster must learn and relearn the areas and the manner in which he is expected to be independent or dependent. If the child begins to return to his reliant behaviors when a "gang" or "lead mentality" exists, the teacher should separate him from those he may follow by redirecting his efforts to more individual work as described earlier in this chapter. If more drastic measures are not needed, the teacher might merely say to the youngster: "I would appreciate your doing this other activity, although I know you chose that one. I would like to see how you handle it." The teacher should choose a task that is interesting to the child but different from that of his peers. He can have the youngster plan to report his own "findings," and perhaps even have him lead a discussion about his new topic. The teacher can also support the youngster's feeling that he can contribute and lead (rather than follow) by setting the stage so he can learn some special skill (e.g., how to mix materials to make soap) and then have him teach the other children. If a new child comes into class, this youngster can be responsible for showing the new child around and getting him oriented to the work.

Whatever the sign of intellectual independence, the teacher should express pleasure so that the youngster will feel that his efforts are recognized as important. How this is done (e.g., when alone or with the group) must take into consideration the risk of embarrassment. When in doubt, it is good to keep in mind that private, realistic praise about self-reliant behavior is always worthwhile, particularly because many overreliant youngsters also display other, more active behavior difficulties in the classroom. Such children often act as if they are independent (e.g., they resist doing what they are told), but when confronted with the need to make decisions about schoolwork do not seem capable of relying upon their own inner resources. If their efforts to take appropriate independent action are ignored because the teacher's attention is drawn only to the more negative, active behaviors, it is unlikely that they will learn or continue to display initiative about academic tasks.

Summary

Overreliance is one of the most stable predictors of success or failure in school at every grade level and in traditional and open class situations. Such behaviors impede learning as much as any other single area of behavior. Whatever the nature of the classroom environment, the teacher must consider and plan for youngsters who are unable to proceed on their own.

Once such a youngster is identified, certain steps can be taken to assure, at the least, that the student is able to start his work. Failure to start work is a major contributor to both academic failure and increased behavioral difficulty. Rather than set sights on work completion and accuracy, it is useful for the teacher to modify initial expectations. The focus must first be upon the issues raised by the child's behavior—his inability to get started, or decide on his own what he will do and how he will do it. Once work is started the youngster can be encouraged to proceed by capitalizing on his need to be reassured by peers as well as adults. Allowing the child opportunities to provide leadership can change his view of his relation to others as well as his ability to work independently. His feelings can be changed from, "They will only like me if I do what they want," to "They like me because I can do well on my own."

How instructions are presented to these youngsters is crucial if they are to make academic progress. Without a clear understanding of what it is the teacher wants him to do, the overreliant child becomes lost and must increasingly seek out others to help him with his work. Even in those educational programs where peers are expected to assist others to figure out problems and carry out work, there is no substitute for the teacher as an instructional leader.

Certain approaches have been found valuable to train children to think on their own, so that they may develop their own internal guidelines. Such approaches provide an atmosphere in which discussing how to proceed is as legitimate as discussing the content to be learned. The youngster can be given opportunities to make choices and to direct his own activities for increasing periods of time. If he shows that he can carry work tasks to completion on his own, then he should be afforded the experience of deciding when and how he will do his work. The experience of self-guidance can eventually make inroads on the youngster's self-image. As he develops the skills to think for himself, and is given opportunities to do so, his picture of his own ability to be successful in school can grow as well.

Footnotes

[1] A. Tribble and R. V. Hall. Effects of peer approval on completion of arithmetic assignments. In F. W. Clark, D. R. Evans and L. A. Hamerlynck (Eds.), *Implementing behavioral programs for schools and clinics: The proceedings of the Third Banff International Conference on Behavior Modification.* Champaign, Illinois: Research Press Co., 1972, 139-140.

[2] G. Spivack and M. Shure. *Social adjustment of young children: A cognitive approach to solving real-life problems.* San Francisco: Jossey-Bass, 1973.

[3] T. C. Lovitt. Self-management projects with children with behavioral difficulties. *Journal of Learning Disabilities,* 1973, *6,* 138-150.

4 Fostering the Student-Teacher Relationship

All behaviors in this dimension show the extent to which the student views the teacher positively and views his relationship with the teacher as warm and friendly. The student indicates by his behavior that he wants to interact with the teacher and that he believes the teacher feels the same about him. He responds in a friendly manner to the teacher, seeks him out before or after class to talk about schoolwork or personal matters, or wants to be physically near the teacher whenever possible.

Young children may touch the teacher, want to have the teacher's arm around them, or offer to do things for the teacher such as running errands, erasing the blackboard, or sharpening pencils. When seeking the teacher's assurance about his schoolwork, he may ask, "Am I right?" or "Is that OK?" not with anxious concern, but with the pleasant anticipation of a positive and supportive teacher reaction. This positive valence is also revealed when teacher praise and concrete external rewards are particularly effective, indicating the teacher's emotional significance to the child. A related behavior occurs when a child tells the teacher about the misbehavior of other children. While this may not be desired, it should be regarded as a natural consequence of the child's identification with the teacher, and not merely as a negative response to a peer's behavior.

The same issues are involved for the older youngster, but a mutuality of relationship is added. Not only does the student show signs of liking the teacher and a willingness to verbalize it, but he manages to evoke a similar response from the teacher. In all instances, the teaching approaches used have significant bearing on the student's continued receptivity to the learning situation and his willingness to express his views and to enter into the learning situation.

Alternative Teaching Strategies

The nature of rapport with the teacher—the extent to which the student's behaviors suggest that the teacher is valued very highly—is of particular importance when considering whether and how the teacher may help a youngster with problems. A commonly held precept in all of the psychoeducational professions wherein people influence other people is that influence can be imparted only after the agent of change (e.g., teacher, friend, therapist) establishes an interpersonal rapport and credibility with the subject (e.g., student, peer, patient). This is true of the relationship between teacher and student, and especially so when the concern is with helping the behaviorally troubled child achieve in the classroom.

Specific teaching approaches and responses to the student can lead him to feel that a relationship with a teacher is possible and is desired. Students have described teachers they most admire as those who "listen" and appear to "understand how you feel," freely give their time, go out of their way to help, are "fair" in dealing with the student, and are friendly and outgoing toward the student. All of these behaviors reflect the teacher's efforts to establish an interpersonal bond and, at least for the behaviorally troubled student, are some of the most important of all teacher behaviors. Also considered important by these students, although

48

secondary in value, is the degree to which the teacher knows the subject, teaches skills well, is secure in himself and likes his job.[1]

However, some teacher responses to a student's efforts to relate are detrimental to rapport. Specific rapport-impeding teacher reactions include those which embarrass the student in front of others, suggest rejection of him as an individual by indicating partiality to favorites, or indicate that the teacher holds a grudge for misbehavior. And a teacher's criticism or threats usually alienate the student.

The teacher's concern for the student is linked to the student's motivation to carry out work tasks. In response to the statement, "I try to do good work in school when . . .," students indicated that their motivation is greatest when the teacher shows a personal interest in them, tends to encourage them rather than "tear down the class and make you feel you're stupid," and when "the teacher likes me and I like my teacher." A major part of the teacher's influence, then, can come from his conscious use of the positive aspects of his personality to foster student efforts.[2]

Particularly when working with youngsters for whom learning is difficult, the teacher must be concerned about what it is he does to foster a relationship with the student. If learning could occur without an interpersonal relationship between student and teacher, then it would be possible to replace man with a programmed machine. As an educator intensely concerned about the nature of the teacher-student relationship, Terry Borton argues that we cannot "teach" any youngster until we "reach and touch" him.

> Stack a man against a machine and immediately the man begins to sound defensive—with good reason. Whatever subject the man teaches the machine can be programmed to teach . . . .
> And yet we, the flesh-and-blood teachers, feel we have something to give. It is not subject knowledge, or even the ability to structure that knowledge according to its more fundamental principles. The machine may do that better than we . . . . What we human teachers have to give, ultimately, is ourselves—our own love for life and for our subject and our ability to respond to the personal concerns of our students.

> We have ourselves to give, and that is a great deal. Within
> any teacher, within any person, there is infinite complexity,
> ability to respond, to exchange ideas, and to change personality.
> The common teacher is not common at all; he is bulging with
> talent, with energy, and with understanding.[3]

For teenagers as well as young children, in regular
classes and classes for the behaviorally troubled child, there is
a significant relationship between the desire to learn and the
feelings the youngster has about the teacher as an approach-
able, friendly and supportive person. If these students are to
develop the motivation to work and to achieve, the teacher
must actively seek to establish a relationship, and to
respond positively to any student overtures. In this process,
the teacher learns something about the youngster as a person
and allows the student to know him as well.

Effective teaching strategies are those that enable the
teacher and the student to learn about each other as real
people with lives and feelings both within and outside of the
classroom. Whether the child is one who reaches out or one
who acts as if he has no need for the teacher, it is necessary
to show a willingness to interact with him. Through actions
as well as words, the teacher must indicate that he is not too
busy with others to have time to work toward establishing
and maintaining a relationship. This can only be accomplished by the clear and frequent display of positive regard
for the child as a person as well as a student. The teacher
must examine his interactions with all of his students to
establish that he is fair and consistent with them. And he
must be flexible enough to assess his approaches in an effort
to identify what he does that might be conducive or detrimental to building an ongoing relationship with a child.

Learning about each other
Some children enter school with-
out having had a warm, personal relationship with an adult
outside of, or even within, their own families. They may not
only be aloof but may also actively show a sense of distrust.

Such a child might not want to be near the teacher or to be touched. He might say directly, or indicate by his behavior, "Leave me alone." This kind of behavior can make any adult feel defensive and wonder, "What's wrong with me?" As one teacher described it: "It can hurt the teacher so much; you've got a child who acts like he doesn't like you. But you have to look beyond that. Somewhere in his background he has not been allowed a warm, personal experience with an adult. He's afraid or insecure or upset about something. You have to recognize that there are some children who seem to resent giving anything of themselves to you. They don't even look at you. They mumble, grunt and talk into their sleeves in response to your questions. If you ask them to do a job they may say no. They respond to your efforts to draw them out with reactions such as, 'What do you want to know for? Why are you so interested?' They act like they don't want to share with you, and that you are only asking to get information to use against them."

To establish that the teacher is open and interested in these youngsters, one approach is for the teacher to talk to the class about himself, his family, and home life. He should encourage all of the children to ask questions ("All the questions you can think of") and then try to have all of the children raise a question. Those with whom rapport is lacking should be looked at, smiled at, and responded to in an especially positive way when they do ask a question. The teacher should indicate to all of the children how pleased he is that they are interested in him. "I know you are interested in me because you have so many questions. We ask a lot of questions because we are interested in finding out about people we like."

This approach can be supplemented by the reading of stories (by the teacher for younger children) that tell about children who want to learn about different people because people are interesting and fun. The children can write their own stories focusing upon themselves, and the teacher should listen to them with interest. Once the child has his "About Me" story completed, if only with his name, address and the names of his brothers and sisters, the teacher can use this information to establish his desire to know the child. The teacher can indicate that "I'm going to think of some questions to ask about you just like the questions the class asked about me." The child can be given the opportunity to pick the question he wants to be asked. The teacher can then write on the blackboard or read to the children all of the questions they asked him earlier. In this way no child feels singled out and each has the chance to think about what he will tell the teacher. Answers should be written as part of the "About Me" story and built upon in a regular and consistent fashion. This establishes that it takes time to get to know others, that the teacher will not lose interest in the youngster as an individual, and that the stories are more than a mere academic exercise.

Establishing fairness and consistency

A child's lack of interest in establishing a relationship with the teacher often reflects his belief that adults promise many things but do not follow through. A report about one such child notes that "in the first grade he adored his teacher, but by the fourth grade he no longer wanted to have anything to do with teachers or school."

Because of the teacher's busy day and the many demands which a class full of children can make, it may be essential to establish specific routines which make it necessary to interact with such distrustful children on a regular basis. Often teachers take the relationship for granted. For example they say, as a routine matter, "You get started and I'll be back in a few minutes" or "I'm really interested in what you're doing," with the best of intentions to return shortly to the child. Circumstances, other children, or forgetfulness may cause failure to follow through. These inconsistencies lead the youngster to feel he cannot depend upon the teacher and that the teacher is "unfair." The youngster is quick to note that the teacher did review another student's work. He feels rejected and often claims that the teacher has favorites or does not like him.

To ensure that there is consistent follow-up and adequate sharing of time, the teacher might set aside a specific "personal discussion time" wherein the child to whom the teacher has promised individual attention will receive it. For the particularly busy teacher, an alarm clock may be set for the same time each day, or the child himself may be asked to tell the teacher when it is "11:45." During these sessions, if only for five minutes, the child for whom relationship building is important should be given the teacher's undivided attention. "This is your time. I just want to be with you. We will do this every day for this week." Once a relationship is established, such stringent, individualized approaches may be discontinued in favor of a more natural interaction during the course of the day. But it will still be necessary to respond frequently and in a way that fosters the child's desire to reach out, to be friendly toward, and to work with the teacher.

Creating an atmosphere of positive feeling

Some teachers talk loudly, do things very quickly, maintain a stern facial expression, or expect answers quickly. They go on to another child if an answer is not forthcoming, or become impatient with the student who is struggling to say something and not "getting it out" (e.g., the child is told to "go back and think about what you want to say"). As one teacher reported, "I didn't realize I was doing things so quickly, and that when the child came close to me it always seemed as if I was in a rush."

Verbal and physical contacts. An increasing number of studies of teaching procedures have tested the effectiveness of teacher-initiated, positive verbal and physical contacts with students. Rapport-building teacher behaviors are generally specified as: (1) praise, provided by saying, for example, "That's good, I'm glad to see you working. That's fine"; (2) physical contact such as patting, holding the child's hand, or hugging his arm; (3) positive facial expressions such as smiling, winking, or nodding at the child; (4) recognizing the child as a positive model by identifying his productive behavior to the class; (5) maintaining emotional closeness by spending time in close physical proximity to the child. Through the use of a combination of these techniques whenever a child's behavior is appropriate to the classroom activities, effective performance of even the behaviorally troubled child can be increased substantially. Although these procedures may appear to require the teacher to spend a great deal of time with the student, this is actually not the case. "Within a ten-second block of time [the teacher] could conceivably praise, wink at, smile at, nod or otherwise socially reinforce many other children as well."[4]

The behaviorally troubled child often perceives his teacher as not liking him.

> Given that this may be true in a few instances, most problem children probably would arrive at this conclusion anyway, since most of their interactions with the teacher are negative. Or, if a teacher only gives a child negative (punishing or reprimanding) attention contingent on inappropriate classroom behavior, what else is the child to think? School principals notoriously are feared and disliked for the same reason. Almost all the principals' interactions with children are the direct result of the child's bad behavior. Thus, by association alone many children not only learn to dislike their teacher and principal, but soon learn to believe the teacher and principal do not like them.[5]

To alleviate this feeling and to foster a positive attitude toward the teacher, the teacher can give "unqualified praise"; i.e., praise that is not an attempt to "extract or encourage continued social behavior." The effort is to indicate that praise is "more than a subtle request for good behavior"; it is a genuine expression of the fact that the teacher is pleased with the child *as an individual.* The child should at times be praised publicly in front of the entire class, particularly when he can serve as a positive model for another child who is misbehaving. The teacher can also express his feelings about the child privately with a "thank you" and a pat on the back.[6]

The teacher can show his desire to respond with positive feelings as part of the regular class activity with little in the way of special planning. For example, instead of merely replying "yes" to the child's request to do something, the teacher might say: "Certainly you may"; or "I'm pleased that you asked, of course you may"; "It makes me feel good that you want to do that. . . ." When "no" is the answer which must be given to a request, the teacher might indicate: "We won't be doing that now, but I will remember you want to." The teacher must then, of course, make every effort to remember. If the child asks to do something that is not possible, the response might be: "That's an interesting idea. Let's get started on this activity first. I will talk with you about your suggestion as soon as we get started." This dialogue affords the teacher another opportunity to know something more about the child as well as to leave him with the feeling that, at the very least, the teacher will listen to his ideas. The child who feels this way about his teacher is more apt to reciprocate when his teacher wishes him to listen and carry out classwork.

For some children it is necessary to create additional teaching methods in order to indicate concretely that the teacher is interested in them. The teacher can set the tone for the day by approaching and complimenting the child when he first takes his seat in the morning, and then continue to initiate positive responses throughout the day.[7] Or, the teacher could tell the child that every 30 minutes he will write from one to ten points in the child's notebook to indicate recognition of his efforts in the classroom.[8]

Allowing the child to express his own feelings and interests. An alternative approach, focusing directly upon the teacher's desire to know about the child's positive feelings, begins with the teacher's telling the children, "Today we are going to have a chance to tell how something gives us a good feeling." The teacher might then present an example of something that gives him a good feeling, such as a personal experience ("I feel good because I . . . .") or an interpersonal experience (". . . because Johnny showed me how to play . . . ."). Each child is encouraged to tell about something that gives him a good feeling. When asked about her feelings, one youngster replied that she felt good because she could ride her bicycle. This afforded the teacher the opportunity to respond: "You can ride your bike, Joyce! I bet that does give you a good feeling. And you look so pretty when you feel good."[9]

It is also useful for the teacher to show interest in the child's own concerns, as well as his classroom accomplishments, by allowing him opportunities to initiate discussion of topics *he* enjoys. The teacher might occasionally (and purposely) allow the youngster to draw the teacher off the topic with his own ideas.

The classroom environment. In addition to using specific alternative teaching strategies that establish a positive link with the student, teachers should be aware that the physical arrangement of the classroom affects their students. Many teachers appear to have no rationale for seating children beyond that of separating potentially disruptive students. Examination of the relationship between physical and social distance in teacher-pupil interactions has shown that students seated in the middle and front of the room felt that "my teacher likes me" more than did youngsters seated in other parts of the room. Furthermore, they showed increased attention and expressed feelings of being "smarter," both of which seem to contribute to a more positive student-teacher interaction.[10] Consequently, for the youngster with whom rapport is lacking, the teacher should not only respond positively, but should also maintain physical proximity in order to establish a relationship with the youngster.

Being open with students. When the teacher, for whatever reason, cannot react positively, he should indicate this openly rather than respond to a child as if the child has done something wrong by approaching him at that time. A teacher could write on the blackboard, "Quiet please, headache," or actually state, "I'm probably going to snap at you if you come up to me because I have a headache." The teacher's behavior then becomes a model for the child in beginning to handle his own feelings. He can see that the teacher can "feel bad" and that, by taking time out, shift mood and return to positive interactions with the class. The teacher can then use this experience as a means of helping the child understand that "It is OK to want to be by yourself or away from the teacher for a time." If such an alert to the teacher's feelings has not been given, all the teacher's earlier promises of "We can always talk," will be undercut by a rebuff of the child's approaches. The youngster may react strongly, feeling threatened, rebuked and let down, and he will continue to be leery or doubtful about his relationship with the teacher. Youngsters often do not understand that people can have good relationships and still have times when they are not close to one another. A perceived rebuke makes them more hesitant about approaching the teacher in the future.

Summary

To establish a relationship with anyone it is necessary to communicate liking and positive interest in many different ways. Especially with children for whom social rapport is difficult, it is necessary to indicate that it is a pleasure to have them around, and that the teacher is willing to linger with them, if only for a moment. Ways to do this can vary from a physical pat, a smile and wink to extended personal discussions. As one teacher commented: "You have to be the kind of teacher who likes to be close to children. You might even give the fellows a tap on the arm or a light push. Older youngsters may not want or understand a hugging kind of affection. With them there are ways to be close without touching such as talking for a moment, telling a secret, whispering a compliment and looking at the student when he is talking to you." All of these reflect that the teacher has time to consider the student as an individual with whom a relationship is valued.

Fostering positive rapport is important not only because it creates a positive environment, but also because it relates to and affects successful academic development. Thus, rapport-building activities and techniques must be seen as a crucial part of the teaching approach and not as an interference with, or an addition to, the teaching of subject matter.

Failure to establish successful relationships with teachers early in a child's school life is all too frequently reflected in his lack of motivation and involvement in later grades. Because prior unsuccessful experiences with adults seem to generalize to others, it is crucial that the child's expression of rejection not be allowed to control the thinking and behavior of the teacher. While it does take time and effort, such a youngster does respond to the overtures of the teacher who indicates that he will neither give up his efforts, nor respond in kind to the child's negative reactions to them.

It is surprising how difficult it is for some teachers to respond positively and show good feelings for youngsters as individuals. This is true in spite of the fact that often relatively little time and effort must be expended to do so. Perhaps they are not willing to allow children to be friendly with them because they feel that if a child learns merely to please adults, he will not develop intrinsic motivation. If this is the reason, the teacher need not worry. The opposite is true; until the child feels he can relate to the teacher, learning is impeded and other troublesome behaviors will occur. Once the child feels that he is liked by his teacher, he is more likely to attempt academic tasks, success at which may then lead to the internal motivation to continue to achieve.

Footnotes

[1] G. Spivack. Behavioral traits that characterize "admired" and "not admired" staff in a residential treatment center, as viewed by male adolescent students. Unpublished manuscript, 1965.

[2] J. R. Frymier. A study of students' motivation to do good work in school. *Journal of Educational Research,* 1964, *57,* 239-244.

[3] T. Borton. *Reach, touch and teach: Student concerns and process education.* New York: McGraw-Hill, 1970, p. 57.

[4] L. Engelhardt, B. Sulzer and M. Altekruse. The counselor as a consultant in eliminating out-of-seat behavior. *Elementary School Guidance and Counseling,* 1971, *5,* 196-204.

[5] C. J. Buys. Effects of teacher reinforcement on elementary pupils' behavior and attitudes. *Psychology in the Schools,* 1972, *9,* 278-288.

[6] Ibid.

[7] A. D. Whitley and B. Sulzer. Reducing disruptive behavior through consultation. *Personnel and Guidance Journal,* 1970, *48,* 836-841.

[8] W. C. Becker, C. H. Madsen, C. R. Arnold and B. A. Thomas. The contingent use of teacher attention and praise in reducing classroom behavior problems. *Journal of Special Education,* 1967, *1,* 287-307.

[9] Borton, pp. 142-143.

[10] A. I. Schwebel and D. L. Cherlin. Physical and social distancing in teacher-pupil relationship. *Journal of Educational Psychology,* 1972, *63,* 543-550.

5 Slowing Down the Impatient, Unreflective Child

Excessive amounts of impatient, unreflective behavior impede learning because the student does not take time to recognize and understand a problem, to give careful thought to proceeding through it, or to maintain an open mind in considering the range of problem solutions. All behaviors in this dimension suggest the youngster's primary tendency to surge forward in his work, as though he cannot or will not tolerate waiting or critically reviewing his own work. It is not the assignment or what is learned from it that is important to him, but the speed with which he can complete it.

These behaviors are revealed in the youngster's approach to academic work requirements. For example, he may start work before getting the directions straight, or start to write or answer before listening to all instructions about how and when to proceed. He hears only the beginning of a set of directions because he has not waited until the end before putting pencil to paper. He often ignores or becomes impatient with details because he feels he has the general idea. "I get it! I get it!!" he shouts, and the teacher feels the impulse to say: "No, wait—I haven't finished—that isn't all—you've forgotten one part." In fact a significant deficiency in this child's functioning is his failure to recognize the relationship of parts to the whole task. Thus, it is characteristic for him to have forgotten or ignored an important aspect of a task, even when claiming, "I'm finished."

In spite of the fact that his work reflects a need for additional instruction and repetition, the impatient child resists going back over material. If the teacher says that the class will spend some time reviewing materials, he is met with strong opposition and lack of interest. The youngster may complain, saying the class has already had that and, "What's the sense of doing it again?" He appears to have little concern with whether the subject matter has been solidly mastered. In a similar fashion, the youngster resists correcting his work. His attention is focused on the belief that he has finished his work, even though he may have rushed through it, making unnecessary mistakes and producing sloppy work. He seems to feel pressured to rush projects through to completion and seek for "what's next."

The teacher will also notice that the youngster acts dogmatic and opinionated, and thus unreceptive to the opinions of others during discussions. The youngster is impatient with any suggestion that he consider multiple viewpoints. He does not wait to hear others out, or even give himself time to think. He retains his own views even when challenged with good arguments. In short, he has great difficulty giving consideration to the views of others, and in modifying his thinking and behavior based upon what others, including the teacher, tell him.

The youngster wants quick "black or white" answers, ones that are simple and uncomplicated. When confronted with choices, none of which is obviously correct or incorrect, his thinking moves quickly to a decision and "closure." The tension of a problem or incomplete task demands quick resolution. If such quick resolution is impossible, the youngster may quit the task, or find some external reasons why he cannot continue. It is as though the child cannot or will not tolerate the anxiety that normally accompanies concern with correctness.

At both the overt behavioral and thinking levels, then, the essential quality of this dimension is a forward surging and seeking for quick solutions. Certainly, some amount of drive toward task completion is necessary and productive, and normal youngsters behave in this manner from time to time. However, excessive amounts of impatient, unreflective behavior are not conducive to learning, and the teacher must plan alternative approaches for dealing with this child.

Alternative Teaching Strategies

To increase the impatient youngster's academic success, the most successful strategies are those that (1) help the youngster focus upon and attend to what is to be done *prior* to taking action; (2) de-emphasize the value of speed at the expense of quality; (3) foster understanding of the need to review and correct work; (4) enable the child to proceed with work in a more thoughtful, patient manner; and (5) encourage planning.

Maintaining attention to directions

It is particularly necessary to have this youngster's attention when addressing him because he is often driven to begin the work after hearing only part of the instructions. The directions must be clear and precise to begin with, in much the same manner as was described for the inattentive child in Chapter 2. The teacher should verbalize the idea that attending to directions is an important task in and of itself, not just important for subsequent activity. "The directions are in front of us, Andy. Tell us, before we do anything, what we are to do."

Some teachers create "attention" and "listening" games where success depends upon listening carefully to the directions. Games may be used in which the child is given a sequence of things to do, for example: (1) go to the door, (2) hop three times, (3) close the window, (4) go back to your seat. Each series is different for each child, thus demanding that careful attention be given to the entire set of directions before proceeding. There are an infinite variety of these sequence games, as well as class lessons dealing with the same content. For example, the timed directions skills test indicates that the child is to "read the entire test before beginning." The last direction on the test is: "Answer only questions 1 and 2." There may be a variety of intermediate directions which interest and challenge the student. For the youngster who did not follow the instruction to read the entire test first, such lessons will alert him to the importance of carefully reading what he is to do before starting work. When necessary, follow-up lessons to such an activity may be designed to further alert the youngster to follow directions carefully. Through these activities, he learns to pay attention to as much detail and information as possible about what must be done before taking action. And he also learns that the end goals can only be known by listening to all of the steps in the directions.

When feasible, the teacher could encourage the youngster to verbalize out loud and then to himself what he must do before he actually does it, and what he must do to avoid troublesome aspects of a problem. The youngster might also be told to write on his paper each step in the directions *before* he makes any attempt to carry out the work. He can then refer to them and should be encouraged to do so. He can also be given problems with incorrect answers and told to find which direction was followed improperly. The child can then restate the directions before making any of the corrections.

All stimuli that suggest action, rather than focusing upon directions, should be eliminated. The teacher could give directions before distributing the materials, or specifically instruct the youngster to put his pencil away, or to "open his eyes and ears" to the teacher to show that he is looking and listening for instructions. Furthermore, the teacher can say to the student: "Remember the game we played where we had to get all of the directions before starting? We are going to do that now too."

Focusing upon directions before carrying them out may be abetted when the teacher allows time for any questions about them, and even encourages thoughtful discussion. "Now it is time to think about the directions and find out if they are clear or not." The teacher may request a student to repeat the directions to another student or to the class, ask if anyone feels something has been left out, or raise a question about them himself (e.g., "What should we do after reading the paragraph?" ". . . after adding the first number?" etc.).

In order to help the child who has particular difficulty waiting for a series of directions, the teacher could assign tasks whose duration will not lead to a build-up of tension over time. Initially short tasks may be assigned, or lengthy tasks divided into independent segments that must be completed before going on to the next segment. For example, the child might be asked to do one or two problems on a page rather than the entire page of problems, with directions given specifically for these problems and not for the others. He should then be required to check these for accuracy in following the directions and should then present his results to the teacher before receiving directions for going on to the next one or two problems. Another child might be required to read only a paragraph from a story and to answer some questions on it, rather than read the entire story and to answer all the questions at the end. The child who has completed a short task could be asked to give directions to another child so that the second child can do the same task. In each instance the youngster is brought to the point of focusing on directions in order to follow them accurately or give them to others.

The short assignment allows the impatient youngster to successfully perceive the relationship between directions and completed task or segment of work. Also, the sequenced task legitimizes the youngster's need for completion, while at the same time pinpointing the relationship between one step and the next in performing larger tasks.

*Communicating
the value of quality over speed*

It is frequently necessary to state explicitly and demonstrate to the youngster the importance of quality over speed of production. A teacher can express concern with neatness because he wants to understand what the student has written. He can show pleasure when the youngster has redone a paper, making it more accurate and legible. These qualities make for pride of accomplishment and should not be avoided as irrelevant to learning.

The teacher must also be aware of his own pacing which might communicate to the youngster the need to rush to completion. The impact of a teacher's own "tempo" on the child's performance has been demonstrated.[1] Among a group of teachers, there is reason to expect that as many as one-third will be highly impulsive themselves, rushing through problems and making a great many errors. Another one-third of teachers are able to take time to think, and make fewer unnecessary errors when confronted with a problem or task. When children in classes with more reflective teachers are followed through the year, it can be seen that they are apt to improve in their own ability to respond patiently. However, children in classes with impulsive teachers show little improvement in their ability to reflect and consider issues before taking action.

The teacher's style of approaching problems makes a real difference to the child's behavior as well as to his learning. The development of a reflective, thoughtful manner of approach is particularly important for such areas of academic achievement as successful reading[2] and reasoning skills.[3] Awareness of the teacher's own style also allows for constructive student placement. Impulsive students have been found to do better when placed with a slower-paced, patient teacher.[4] And with knowledge of his own style, each teacher can work to modify his own pace by practicing the instructions for himself which are being used to aid children who are impulsive, as described later in this chapter (see also Chapter 7, Promoting Relevant Talk).

As suggested earlier, an underlying aspect of this behavior dimension is a pressure for action. These youngsters have often been characterized as having a fast inner clock that races along. For impatient people a wait of 10 minutes is subjectively equal to that of a more patient person who waits 15 minutes. The teacher may instruct the child in the proper way to respond to assignments, emphasizing that there is plenty of time to complete the tasks. "There's no need to rush. If you don't finish today you can do so tomorrow. Just do whatever you do well. Do it correctly and properly. That's what's important." The emphasis should be on working slowly and carefully. "Before we say we are finished, I want everyone to think about the work. Did you answer the questions correctly? Did you take the time to make everything neat and readable? No hands, please. I don't want an answer. I only want you to think about what you are doing. I will call on you and we will check it over."

The specific issue of time must often become a focus of attention for the teacher in creating strategies. Time is important as it relates to the pacing of what is to be done and enough time must always be allowed so there is no issue of urgency. "Clock time" thus becomes a useful educational device. The impatient youngster may be told how much time he should spend on an assignment. A big clock may be set on the teacher's desk if there is not a wall clock. Experience with clock time in relation to work suggests that it helps correct the fast inner clock, and consequently reduces the pressure the youngster feels to move quickly into action. Instructions might be: "You should use 20 minutes to work on that lesson. See how much time you take and see if you have time left over. If you do, then you worked too fast." The youngster working with the feedback from clock time usually discovers he has more time than he felt he would, and comes to view time not as a source of pressure, but as a context and guide which he can use to regulate action. The teacher might ask the youngster, "What does it mean when you have time left over?" The aim is to help him realize that completing his work with clock time remaining means that he has worked too quickly and must, in the next work session, work more slowly. If work is completed appropriately, then tasks can be increased to provide him with the opportunity to test his ability to follow more directions without rushing. The idea is to increase the number of directions and amount of work rather than decrease the time taken to complete the work.

This youngster may also be helped by providing him with physical activities that emphasize training tension control, or the slow discharging of tension over time. Games such as "statue," modern dance, or Yoga are examples of activities in which regulation of muscle tension is crucial; they temper the quick release typical of such youngsters. The ability to wait, to contain tension while thinking out what must be done and how, is the issue.

Focusing upon review

It has been noted that the youngster resists reviewing what he has done, thus exercising insufficient check on his work. Teachers often must consider strategies to combat such resistance and the youngster's tendency not to look back self-critically on what he has done. In overcoming this tendency it is sometimes necessary for the teacher to take the youngster back to his work, individually, with immediate and detailed feedback. General statements or accusations about sloppiness or incorrectness, and lectures about how the youngster's work underestimates his "true" ability are of little avail. It is necessary, at least initially, to go over his work with him, pointing out where there are errors, how rushing led to his missing the point, and where obvious care did lead to good results.

Some teachers report that it is helpful to have the youngster read or describe what he has done when he is finished with an assignment, and then read or restate what was asked. Together, the teacher and student can evaluate the finished product in relation to the initial directions or the goal stated at the start. Ultimately, the youngster should be able to go over his own work while the teacher watches;

switching roles with the teacher, the youngster "plays" the teacher for himself. Having the youngster find his own mistakes and correct them can even become an interesting and pleasant task, especially with both the praise and pride that evolves with an improved end product. Some teachers have suggested "proofreading" sessions wherein students correct each other's spelling or grammar, each youngster focusing on lack of clarity or care in production, as well as what he has learned by reviewing the work.

The teacher should emphasize specifically, whenever possible, that time given to review is a legitimate part of the time spent in producing work, and not to be used only when something is wrong. This can be concretized in the classroom when the teacher indicates the time to be spent upon original production of an assignment, and then specifies the time to be spent upon self-critical reivew and corrections. For instance: "We will spend a few minutes getting the directions straight, then we will spend at least 20 minutes on the problem; after that we will spend another 20 minutes rereading and checking our work." Youngsters generally are not taught the habit of review in an orderly fashion, but the necessity of it for impatient youngsters is clear.

Another useful alternative strategy to help the impatient youngster is to record with him the nature of his work over a period of time. The youngster may be encouraged to keep his own file of his work in a notebook on his desk. While useful for other purposes, ongoing examination of completed work has specific value in engendering self-critical review. It creates a "history" to look back upon, a record of successes and failures, and of change. The child can contrast past products with his present state of progress. Most youngsters can be brought to talk about past performance when confronted with evidence of their work over time, often with surprising insights. One child indicated, "When I compare these two papers, I can see how I thought about what I was doing on this one. On this one I was rushing."

Impatient, unreflective youngsters need immediate feedback about their work. Their rushing through work may be evidence of the extent to which they value end products because they signify that the task is completed and tension reduced. Since these youngsters respond well to external rewards and teacher response to what they do, the teacher should initially provide an immediate response to their completed work, aimed at keeping them focused on the work. If the youngster finishes early, the teacher should review his product with him, making the review part of the work. During the review it is important to point out the good qualities as well as errors or issues missed, and ways to improve, saying for instance: "What do the directions say to do here? How much time should you take to do this work?" Praise after the child returns to his work is particularly important. Displaying the youngster's "improved" product is particularly effective in helping him to appreciate the fact that a good correction is as valued as a good first effort.

Equally important to praise for many of these youngsters is teacher verbalization about how the teacher himself always looks back over his work when he finishes to make sure he has not missed something, or how he makes sure his papers or projects are done with care. This is valuable because it spells out to the child the specific behaviors he may imitate to become more thoughtful like the teacher. The youngster watches the teacher as the teacher looks at his end product, and hears the teacher talk about it in relation to previous directions and goals. The reflective teacher who verbalizes his own cautions in his own work helps such children become less impatient. The reflective teacher who displays behaviors indicating that his work is well planned and that he is willing to "take his time" provides a constructive model for these children (see information above on teacher tempo).

Educating reflectiveness
The impatient behavior of these youngsters suggests a cognitive style characterized by quickly jumping to conclusions, insufficient consideration of alternative solutions to problems, and general lack of planning about

what is to be done. This pattern of deficiency often must be dealt with by making specific plans to train thinking. Without such strategies the impulsive and impatient behavior of some children cannot be meaningfully affected.

To affect these deficiencies in thought requires a style of teaching which may be employed regardless of the content. One facet of this style is the focus on alternatives. The goal is to have the youngster see that there is more than one possibility in a situation, more than one possible answer or means to an end. A class discussion about history may focus on how different events *might* have occurred; a mystery story might be handled on the basis of how many *different* endings are *possible;* a planned class visit may focus on the different ways the class (or the impatient youngster) might travel to the destination and what to look for so they can return without getting lost. During storytelling with young children, the story may be interrupted with the question: "Let's see how many ways we can think of to help Mary get what she wants in the story." In all of these, the focus with the youngster is on his generating alternate possibilities, not the "right" or acceptable answer. Emphasis is on the different ways to do something, not on getting it done. Classroom discussions provide the teacher with a variety of opportunities to ask, "What else could she do?" or "Let's find all the reasons we can to explain what happened."

The teacher's response to ideas suggested by the students must reflect his willingness to accept alternatives. His response to each idea should be, "That's another good idea. Let's keep thinking of good ideas." Specific techniques to help young children develop the ability to see alternatives and to appreciate consequences have been developed. The following is an example of one approach. Prior to beginning an assignment (or at the point where the student expresses an unwillingness to go over his work) the teacher can say to him, "Let's try to think of as many ways as we can to make sure that the work is done correctly. What is one way . . . ?" Following each student's reply, the teacher should respond by writing his words on the board and stating, "That's an idea.

That's one way. Can you think of another way? Let's think of different ways." The purpose is to guide the youngster in thinking about and articulating his own alternatives, rather than having the teacher tell him what to do. Once this is done, the teacher can ask the student to tell what might happen if he follows the first alternative. In this manner the impatient youngster is helped to reflect on alternative actions he might take, and to see his actions in terms of possible consequences.[5]

The teacher can also use a "fading procedure" to get the impatient youngster to slow down and think first before working on problems. To carry out the procedure, the steps to be followed require that the teacher (1) actively do a task, saying out loud the steps and methods used, while the child watches; (2) have the child repeat the same task while he repeats the instructions aloud; (3) have the child work alone, giving himself instructions out loud; (4) have the child continue to work on the task while whispering or moving his lips to give instructions to himself; and (5) have the child work without anything said aloud. This approach is based on the notion that the "internalization of verbal commands is a critical step in the child's development of voluntary control of his behavior."[6] While this approach is considered an effective procedure with impatient, unreflective children, it may be utilized with a variety of youngsters whose behavior is characterized by impulsiveness or lack of thought before action. (See Chapter 7, Promoting Relevant Talk; and Chapter 10, Meeting the Needs of the Restless, Socially Overinvolved Student.)

The following is an example of the fading procedure which successfully increased the time the children took to make a decision and simultaneously decreased impulsive responding. As in the outline above, first the teacher and then the child repeated these directions while working.

> Okay, what is it I have to do? You want me to copy the picture with the different lines. I have to go slow and be careful. Okay, draw the line down, down, good; then to the right, that's it; now

down some more and to the left. Good, I'm doing fine so far. Remember go slow. Now back up again. No, I was supposed to go down. That's okay. Just erase the line carefully. . . . Good. . . . Even if I make an error I can go on slowly and carefully. Okay I have to go down now. Finished. I did it.[7]

In this example the teacher deliberately made an error and handled it by stating and showing, "Just erase carefully . . . . Even if I make an error I can go on slowly and carefully." Approaching the issue of correcting errors is extremely important for impatient children because they resist going over work to make corrections, and when they do attempt to make changes, their work becomes sloppy and messy. Their work is more likely to deteriorate following errors.

This fading approach can be adapted to most academic levels and tasks (e.g., doing arithmetic problems, drawing maps, learning letters of the alphabet, etc.), but the format for learning self-instruction to work slowly and correct mistakes would be the same. This procedure should be used for a variety of tasks to provide enough repetition to allow the process to become automatic.

A second set of instructions to aid the child to develop a strategy for approaching tasks is exemplified in the following sequence. The task is to select the form which matches a standard form. The teacher indicates that the way to proceed is to say and think:

I have to remember to go slowly to get it right. Look carefully at this one. . . , now look at these carefully . . . . Is this one different? Yes, it has an extra leaf. Good, I can eliminate this one. Now, let's look at this one . . . . I think it's this one, but let me first check the others. Good, I'm going slow and carefully. Okay, I think it's this one.[8]

Once again it is suggested that the teacher show and tell the child how to think about, cope with and correct errors. The child must be exposed to a model who demonstrates how to search for the proper answers by eliminating incorrect ones, by making comparisons among details, and by looking at all aspects of a problem before answering. If specific attention must be paid to correcting errors, the teacher might say and then teach the child to say, "It's OK, just be careful. I should have looked more carefully. Follow the plan to check each one. Good, I'm going more slowly."[9] Notice that the teacher does not say, "You should have looked more carefully," but rather first talks to himself about his own behavior and then teaches the child to do the same.

The teacher should exercise care when using this procedure with non-impatient children, who may interpret the instructions to go slower as indicating that they were not doing well. This procedure may lead to a decrease in the performance of the child who does not need to slow down. However, use of this procedure up to now has helped impulsive children to slow down, "taking their time . . . improving their performance."[10]

Encouraging planning

Encouraging and training the child in planning his own work aids the attainment of all of the teaching goals described in this chapter: getting the details before acting, attending to quality, reviewing, and becoming more patient and thoughtful. This may require helping the child to make lists or draw how things should be begun and how they should be when finished. Charts, pictures and calendars may be used, constructed by the youngster when possible, showing what he wants to do and when. In the planning of assignments, he may need to be helped to state what he wants to do, what steps to follow, and even when he wants to reach each step along the way. Encouraging the student to verbalize his own plans at each step is essential.

Meeting with the impatient student beforehand about the amount of work he plans to do during a given period of time, then meeting periodically with him within this time to discuss progress or problems and how to overcome them, is often necessary. It is also useful to review a completed project to point out how plans actually worked out. The focus is not on the quality of the end product per se, but on how the youngster can relate what he wants to accomplish to how he is going to proceed with it. It is also important, as in all dealings with the impatient child, for the teacher to make certain that his own manner of proceeding does not contradict the more planful method he is attempting to teach.

Summary

Learning requires the ability to wait for information, to think about how to proceed when given directions, and then to work at a pace which allows time for careful reflection upon what is being done. It is not surprising that a child who responds impatiently has difficulty gaining academic success. Such a child, while often not disruptive or apt to interfere with the work of others, clearly needs the assistance of the teacher if he is to regulate his impulse to charge forward without looking back. Special plans must be designed for some of these youngsters whether their impulsive behavior is a response to the present classroom environment or reflects a method of thinking which has evolved over a period of time.

Of particular importance in aiding this youngster is the teacher's style of approach. Whether experienced or inexperienced, teachers who demonstrate a thoughtful approach have a greater chance of helping the child to develop such an approach as well. When programming for these youngsters, the teacher should refrain from such pitfalls as the temptation to motivate children by stating, "Let's see who can be the first one done."

The problem for the child is not in getting the work done. It is important to recognize that he does want to get started and to finish assignments. The problem is that when left on his own he rushes through the work before getting the directions straight, thereby making mistakes that he probably would not have made had he approached the task in a more thoughtful manner. For him completion, not correctness, equals success. When a task is done he may feel a sense of relief and even look for new work ("What do I do next?"). The teacher should emphasize that success may be gained in a number of ways: "Success is getting the directions straight; success is following all of the directions correctly; success is going slowly to be sure; success is taking my time."

Another impediment to learning, resistance to review, may be lessened through the use of techniques concerned with time. These youngsters often have what has been called a fast inner clock. It is frequently helpful to afford the child the opportunity to complete a short amount of work and then immediately to check his work before going on to the next task. These short time assignments allow the teacher the opportunity to head off errors so that when the youngster goes back over his work he sees how well he has done, and does not have to spend a long period of time trying to redo his old mistakes. This allows him to feel proud when reviewing with the teacher and minimizes the tendency for his work to deteriorate as errors increase. It is less likely that a child will comfortably return to look over work that he feels has many errors. Furthermore, he is more likely to feel he can work with a teacher who takes the time to review successful work. Whether work is correctly done or not, helping these youngsters to learn about the importance of review is a step in the direction of behaviors conducive to academic success.

Strategies which teach ways to think about and approach work assignments have had particular success in slowing down the impatient child. One set of techniques is based on the premise that a child can be taught the methods to work slowly and with patience by the teacher explaining and demonstrating in a specific way the desired thoughtful behavior. A second viewpoint asserts that a child learns to behave more effectively following training in which the child himself is guided to articulate alternative ways to handle a situation, rather than by observing or listening to a teacher who tells and shows him what to think and do. Thus, rather than suggest to the child, "Here's how to behave, watch me and then you do it," the teacher might ask the child to think of his own way to make sure he has the directions straight. In both cases, the intent is to teach the child the habit of thinking in ways which enable him to guide his own behavior.

Finally, as is the case throughout this book, the ultimate aim is to provide the teacher with techniques to use that enable the child to function as independently as possible as a learner in the classroom. The evidence is that many impatient children can be helped by the thoughtful teacher.

Footnotes

[1] R. M. Yando and J. Kagan. The effect of teacher tempo on the child. *Child Development,* 1968, *39,* 27-34

[2] J. Kagan. Reflection-impulsivity and reading ability in primary grade children. *Child Development,* 1965, *36,* 609-628.

[3] J. Kagan, L. Pearson and L. Welch. Conceptual impulsivity and inductive reasoning. *Child Development,* 1966, *37,* 359-365.

[4] J. Kagan. Reflection-impulsivity: The generality and dynamics of conceptual tempo. *Journal of Abnormal Psychology,* 1966, *71,* 17-24.

[5] G. Spivack and M. Shure. *Social adjustment of young children: A cognitive approach to solving real-life problems.* San Francisco: Jossey-Bass, 1974.

[6] D. H. Meichenbaum and J. Goodman. Training impulsive children to talk to themselves: A means of developing self-control. *Journal of Abnormal Psychology,* 1971, *77,* 115-126.

[7] Ibid.

[8] Ibid.

[9] Ibid.

[10] Ibid.

6 Increasing Initiative and Involvement

The essence of this dimension is the quality of the young-ster's personal, active and positive involvement in the process of learning. It reflects the extent to which he interacts with others about ideas, and introduces his own personal experiences and creations in a fashion which enriches the learning of everyone involved. What goes on in the classroom is not compartmentalized or alien to what goes on during the rest of the youngster's life. The child's outside experiences and school experiences become one because he involves himself in his learning.

Examining initiative from the vantage point of a developmental stage, Erikson has stressed its importance:

> There is in every child at every stage a new miracle of vigorous unfolding, which constitutes a new hope and a new responsibility for all. Such is the pervading quality of initiative. . . the child suddenly seems to "grow together" both in his person and his body. He appears "more himself," more loving, relaxed and brighter in his judgment, more activated and activating. He is in free possession of a surplus of energy which permits him to forget failures quickly and to approach what seems desirable (even if it also seems uncertain and dangerous) with undiminished and more accurate direction. Initiative adds to autonomy the quality of undertaking, planning and "attacking" a task. . . .

> . . . man needs a sense of initiative for whatever he learns
> and does, from fruit-gathering to a system of enterprise.[1]

Within the classroom the two major elements in this dimension are reflected in particular student behaviors. The first element is the youngster's contribution of his personal experiences to the learning interaction. He may bring things from home that relate to classwork. When he tells a story, it reflects his own imagination and is of interest because it adds something personal and therefore a unique touch. Talk is not mere intellectualization. It reflects an interlacing of knowledge and personality. The readiness to engage in verbal interchange is complemented by a personal openness and engagement with others.

The second element is the youngster's active participation in classroom activities by initiating interchange, asking questions to get answers, contributing answers, and volunteering information. He readily enters into a give and take of ideas, brings up different points of view, and uses the ideas of others as a springboard for the sharing of his own ideas. He asks "Why?" as part of a reciprocal interchange with students and teacher.

The youngster who displays these two elements—personal involvement in the learning process and active participation in classroom activities—is frequently recognized as creative. He presents original or unique ideas which are relevant during discussions. Assignments or projects are prepared in interesting and original ways. In discussions the youngster suggests alternate possibilities or more than one solution to a problem. His involvement and ease in the classroom not only allow him to put his personal stamp on what he does, but are accompanied by an open-mindedness toward the variety of possibilities in any problem situation.

Alternative Teaching Strategies

In contrast to students who display involvement and initiative in the classroom are students who are passive receivers in the educational process. A substantial number of youngsters in almost every classroom display little active engagement in what is going on. Since they may reveal no behavioral problems, they may easily be overlooked. In fact, some teachers may encourage such passive behavior, mistaking it for the mark of a good student, or simply because it causes less trouble. Whatever the reason, however, learning is impeded by lack of involvement.

Personal involvement and initiative in the learning process, however manifest, almost invariably suggest that the youngster is making something out of his educational experiences. Techniques that encourage such involvement thus become particularly important to the teacher.

Relating school to the child's world
What makes a youngster involve himself and take initiative in the classroom—and what makes him view school as a meaningful part of his total life—is a complex process dependent upon many forces, both at school and at home.

There can be little doubt that the attitude and involvement of parents in their child's schooling play a significant role in determining the child's desire and willingness to relate himself to school. Beyond the effect of the parents' general approach to ideas and problems, the child will have much to overcome in any attempt to involve himself positively at school if school is spoken of in derogatory ways, teachers are criticized, or education is demeaned in the home. It is little better, though perhaps somewhat less detrimental, when school is never discussed at all. In many homes the child's school activities are not discussed, and in fact little discussion between parent and child takes place. Whether by negative actions or none at all, the parents do not support the idea of school as an approved part of a child's life.

It is easiest for the child to involve himself when school and home life are meshed, when parents play an active role in and around the school, when conversation about school is as natural as talk about family recreation, parent employment, or household chores, and when parents show enthusiasm about the child's obtaining a good education. The child who is active or involved in other aspects of his life may not be so in school largely because the relationship between school and non-school has not been supported by significant adults.[2]

A talk with the youngster's parents may help all concerned in several ways. Some parents are not aware that their youngster's level of involvement relates to his achievement in classroom work. Many parents do not realize that teachers value active participation by the child. For some parents the overriding concern is that their child be obedient and do what he is told. They have the opinion that children learn by listening to the teacher, and that children who are talking cannot be listening.

Once the importance of involvement is pointed out, most parents want to help their children involve themselves and will respond to the teacher who reaches out to them. However, even though motivated, many parents do not know what they can then do to help. Leadership must be assumed by the teacher. One way to encourage parental involvement is to arrange a series of meetings over time, perhaps each month or two, not on the basis of a "problem" but as a means of cross-checking with one another about progress in carrying out a specific plan. Following a series of such meetings, one mother commented:

> I now realize you can suppress a child's involvement and curiosity when he's young and he won't have any later on. If he wants to ask you something or tell about school he might think, "No, she's not interested. I won't bother." If they can't tell you about school when they're young they're never going to. Then you won't have any idea what they're doing.[3]

Beyond supporting parents' efforts to talk with their child, the teacher must focus upon specific ways parents can help the youngster become more involved by involving themselves in school-related activities. Putting parents in this "helping" role lessens defensive feelings. Specific suggestions

82

might include reading a series of stories to the child at home, helping him with a special project that relates to school, supplying materials or suggestions for projects, or listening to the child and responding to his questions. The parent might be encouraged to set aside a time, for instance at dinner, for listening to the child when he wants to tell about happenings at school.

The parent should also be made aware of the value of attending and participating in school events which are open to parents. The teacher can also help parents by keeping them informed of events in the community that relate to school and that the parents would be especially interested in as an activity for their youngster. At times special television programs, movies, museum exhibits, science fairs, or sporting events provide an opportunity for parents to become involved with their youngster in a school-related activity, which the teacher can then follow up in a class discussion. A parent may need and should get encouragement to take his child to the local public library on a scheduled basis. Many parents neglect these matters not out of indifference but because they do not appreciate how their positive involvement encourages their child's involvement.

Such working out of a mutual plan grows into parental involvement, frequently with positive effects for the child's participation in the classroom. The youngster sees the parent at school, or knows his parents are meeting with his teacher. Often a child is particularly impressed when the parent reports something positive the teacher has said about him (e.g., "How well you took part in the discussion about....") and when the parent relates certain aspects of what he and the teacher have discussed (e.g., "We are wondering if you would bring in your collection and tell the class about it"). It is important for this feedback to be positive, and to center on something the child is doing or has done, or something that is coming up that he will like. Parental interest and involvement are shown in the context of positive feelings, and these in combination produce optimal results. The parents' interest is seen by the child as approval of his own involvement and gives him reason to desire "belonging" in school and sharing with others there.

Expanding the child's
view of himself in his world

Beyond involving the home in what happens at school, it is often helpful to provide the child with direct experiences which relate schoolwork to events in his outside community. Such activities become particularly important when parental involvement is not feasible.

The field trip provides the child with experiences which can be talked or written about in class. Before departing on a field trip special effort must be made to direct the under-involved student to look for certain things to show, and to discuss what he will see. For example, youngsters may be shown pictures or models of machines and then be taken to a factory or newspaper plant. Each would know he is to report to the class after the trip about how the machinery produced the product. A television or staged format can be used to increase interest by allowing the child to show as well as to tell about what he saw. The child may be asked to bring in a sample or to make a chart, script or diagram to give him something special to show and talk from. In this way, the youngster's outside experience gives him definite ideas and things to present, and an opportunity to share that experience as something particular of his with his classmates.

During the field trip, it is valuable to take pictures, particularly of the under-involved child. These pictures can be used as starting points for discussion. The youngster may be shown a picture of himself in front of an interesting display and asked, "When did this take place? What were you doing in this picture? Tell us what was going on then." Through these techniques the youngster becomes aware of and involved in relating his "outside" personal experiences to the classroom.

84

Relating school to the child

Most efforts to involve a student are initiated by the teacher in order to stimulate the child's interests and to spark his desire to contribute to class projects and discussions. While some youngsters may respond following parent-teacher meetings or to the excitement of a field trip, others may need to be reached more personally before they can open up in class. To involve such a youngster, it is often essential that the teacher find out about his particular interests both outside and inside school, so that these may be related to the goals of the classroom.

The more "informal" and activity-centered the classroom setting, the more the child is given a choice in selecting the details of his work, the easier it will be for the teacher to discover what intrinsically interests the child. As a bridge to involvement it is a useful strategy to use varied media materials. The more diverse the materials in the classroom, the easier it is to discover interests through watching the youngster choose one activity over another. Beyond observation of the child the teacher might make use of creative media to learn about him. The child may be asked to draw a picture from a story or program he liked and asked to tell about it. Every youngster has something in his own mind when he draws a picture, models clay or builds a tower, and these products help him describe his interests. They become an objective "thing" which the child can talk about without the inhibitions that would come into play if he were asked directly to express his own thoughts.

Another method to discover important information about a youngster's life beyond the classroom is the "personal time line" technique.[4] This teaching device is often used in social studies to foster understanding of the place of events in history. In this case, the child is taught to create his own personal time line by placing important events in his life along a line in order from the earliest (e.g., birth) to the present and even into the future, indicating when they occurred; he might later talk about them in class discussion. Some children become even more involved in this process by drawing pictures of important events (e.g., my first baseball game, when my new baby sister came to the family, etc.) or bringing in materials and pictures to paste on the time line. This technique not only affords the teacher insights normally not revealed by a reticent child; it also shows the child that self-interest can be a vital part of academic learning.

Once a child has created his own personal time line, he can be encouraged to expand upon it. He can add events relevant to school to correspond with events in his life. The teacher might provide almanacs for each year of the child's life and ask him to look up information to relate to his time line. The child can then be encouraged to create new time lines that correspond to his age but for another period of time. For example, the child can be told: "You are eight years old. Ask your mother to tell you about herself so you can make a time line for her when she was eight years old." Younger children, just learning numbers and reading skills, can carry out the procedure by being given magazines and instructed to "pick out pictures that tell about the big fire that happened on your street in the fall," to be put on the line. These children can be assisted to focus attention upon academically relevant materials with such instructions as "find or draw a picture of the men going to the moon and add it to your line." Through these procedures the under-involved youngster is given a means to initiate ideas and personal interests as part of a relevant classroom activity.

Another way a teacher can work directly with the youngster to help him relate his life and interests outside school to the classroom is by having him carry out a specific, special assignment: to bring in a certain picture, story, or object in which he has expressed interest. When something is brought in, the teacher can highlight its value, either as it pertains to a topic being studied or simply as the child's contribution to the class. This procedure becomes a "show-and-tell" experience. It is very important, however, that what is brought in be of special interest to the child, rather than a mere reflection of the teacher's desire to draw the child into the group. The concern is with helping the child relate himself to school, and thus his interests are of paramount importance.

Increasing involvement with work and with others may also be accomplished by carrying out group projects which capitalize upon what the child likes. The projects can involve the entire class or a smaller group. Each child is asked to contribute something from home; each contribution may be minor, but is important to the success of the total project. For example, the child may like a particular food and choose a recipe he wants to make. The ingredients and utensils may be listed during group discussion. The under-involved child can be encouraged: "Without your contribution, we can't make this." If necessary the teacher might help him obtain what he must bring in, although it is preferable that the parent do this. When the food is finished, this youngster may be the first to taste it, and asked why he likes or dislikes it.

The teacher may find it necessary to provide added structure for the youngster by following up knowledge of his interests. He can be given something to explore at home. When he returns to school, he should be encouraged to share with the class what he has discovered.

Creating an atmosphere
to encourage involvement

In addition to the attempts to create circumstances that relate the youngster's school life to his life outside of the classroom, specific strategies are necessary to create an atmosphere which encourages the sharing of experiences and thoughts with others. Since these youngsters are not prone to enter into classroom discussion, they miss opportunities for an exchange of views and dialogue. For many youngsters free verbal exchange is inhibited because they feel they will not be listened to, or fear being embarrassed, belittled, corrected or criticized. For these children, the acceptability of what they say has been overemphasized. Their willingness to attempt to exchange ideas and the implicit desire for interpersonal involvement has been ignored to the detriment of the child and his involvement in the learning environment. Reticence further impedes learning because the youngsters do not perfect their ability to raise questions or to put ideas into words.

To increase the child's involvement, the teacher should respond enthusiastically to the child's comments. A recent study showed that teachers who do respond enthusiastically to what a child says have far greater frequency of student-initiated comments than those who give no feedback, disapprove or indicate that what the child says is unacceptable.[5]

> Apparently one of the major difficulties in applying the principle of showing children that their ideas have value is that in the minds of many teachers and adults there is considerable doubt as to the worth of children's ideas—they honestly do not believe that children are capable of producing ideas that have value. If the teacher holds such a belief, whether knowingly or unknowingly, he will not be effective in putting this principle into practice. We can only suggest that people who are unconvinced as to the value of children's ideas keep an open mind and try to assess objectively the novel productions of young people.[6]

One step which may have to be taken to overcome a child's reticence is to establish a one-to-one bridge between the youngster and teacher. A discussion may focus on information from the child's time line and classroom observation, and from discussions with parents about his interests and hobbies, what he does at home and what his parents do with him. The goal is twofold: to help him feel comfortable about the exchange of ideas; and to indicate that it is appropriate for him to involve himself by expressing his own ideas and interests, and not merely to react to those of the teacher. It is crucial that the youngster not feel pressured and that what he says be received positively, without critical comment or implied need for correction. The approach requires that the teacher be a good listener, asking questions only to draw out the child's thoughts without passing judgment in any way. If the teacher asks a question, it is to gain more information and not to express an opinion. A discussion is fostered when the teacher responds: "I see what you mean—Oh yes, now I understand," or "That was interesting—I never knew that," or "I never realized how interested you are in rocks." If such talk and information-gathering serve their purpose, a transition can be made from this to the youngster's talking in class: "Maybe someday you might want to tell the class about your rock collection."

Even if such a youngster begins to interact with the teacher and express himself fairly well in a safe adult relationship, the transition to discussion with the peer group often requires a gentle push and continued teacher support. A useful first step is to move him into a small group of friends or youngsters with a similar interest, the goal being a group report. The youngster may be asked to talk about the results of the discussion. Whatever his particular role, however, the small group is easier for most youngsters to relate to, and can also create the gentle pressure for all to interact which may be missing in the class as a whole. If the teacher observes the group in action, he may draw out the youngster with a question, or provide the added support that may be needed: "Do you want to tell us about something? It looked like you might."

In ensuing general classroom discussions, it is often possible for the teacher to bring the child into an interchange by referring to something the child has talked about in other circumstances or by acknowledging an idea as his. His opinion may be sought directly when discussion turns to something known to be of particular interest to him.

Care must be taken in considering the pace with which the youngster is drawn out. Sometimes it is easier for a youngster initially to participate through an activity where verbalization is kept to a minimum, or is not the essential ingredient. For instance, he may participate in an activity by taking pictures of it with a Polaroid camera. Such a child often is able to participate more freely if playing someone other than himself. He can play a part in a play or puppet theatre, or he can act and wear a costume.

A useful approach to encourage self-expression is the "Magic Net" exercise. The children are provided with 36" by 72" pieces of different-colored nylon net they can use to cover themselves. In groups of six to ten they are asked to play a person, animal or anything they may wish to become. The children may pantomime, dance or walk the characters. Others in the class are encouraged to make up a story for the players to act out. Some children may choose to play the same role chosen by others; e.g., if one girl chooses to be a queen, all girls may follow suit. Even with the "protection" of the Magic Net, it can be difficult for these youngsters to act alone. Since one purpose of this activity is to create an atmosphere that fosters involvement, children can be allowed to choose the same role as a means of providing one another support. When a child chooses a unique role, support should be provided if necessary by encouraging others to play that role with the child:

> Pamela had been so quiet and had not been a part of the creative drama, dance, song, or play until today. She was given a "Magic Net" and decided to be a bear. She was too timid and withdrawn to be a good bear, even with encouragement. Dr. Torrance, realizing this, reinforced her with some more bear children. She became an excellent bear. She overcame her shyness and began to interact with the group, not just in play-acting. Her success seemed to change her whole self-image. Pamela, with her quiet voice, entered into the group problem-finding game and gave very intelligent problems. She was anxious to participate and to contribute to the group... I saw a sense of achievement in her approach.
>
> ... I found today that she is far more intelligent than I had dreamed. She lacks confidence, and being unsure and inhibited can be taken for signs of low intelligence. But when the inhibition is broken, you can see that she is not dull but just too afraid to exert and show her abilities.[7]

Providing such experiences is crucial, particularly if the youngster hesitates becoming involved because he feels that he has nothing to share. Each time he refuses or fails, it diminishes his feeling that he is able to, or even wants to share his experiences with others. Children who hold back and display little involvement or initiative might be telling the teacher, through these behaviors, "I am too unsure about what I think to decide what to say on my own so I will talk only when I am asked to." Through the use of techniques like those described above, these children are reassured that the teacher will not let them be hurt or feel foolish, and will guide them to success.

Encouraging the verbalization of ideas

Closely associated with techniques that encourage classroom involvement are specific techniques that encourage the child to verbalize his ideas more freely. A common point of concern in these techniques is to avoid the issue of "right and wrong," focusing instead upon how many different or unusual ideas are possible in a given situation. After reading stories or examining pictures and materials, students could be asked to (1) think of as many ideas as you can about. . . (e.g., what is happening; what might happen if fish lived on land, or it were illegal to sing); (2) ask as many questions as you can to find out what is happening in the picture; (3) think of as many ideas as you can for unusual uses for. . . (e.g., junk automobiles, broken hula hoops, worn out frisbees).

Such basic training in creative problem-solving increases the expression of ideas in relatively brief periods of time. These approaches may be followed by similar activities and discussions where the idea is to verbalize about and resolve some real issue in the lives of the students. These procedures not only have helped the students to increase their ability to produce original ideas, but have also had general effects on their learning ability. Involvement increases, as does their ability to keep on with a task in spite of obstacles. Children express more interest in the world around them, and show willingness to try to find out more about it.[8]

Children should also be encouraged to generate and verbalize their own ideas about how to solve typical interpersonal problems, and possible consequences of each solution. Some of the techniques which enhance reflectiveness (see Chapter 5) are also useful in stimulating verbalization in class. The focus is on getting children in small groups to generate all the possibilities in a given situation (e.g., what a child might do or say to get a toy another child is playing with, or to get another child to play with him). The approach may even be broadened to include such questions to the group as: "What might you do or say so that others in class would know about a trip you just took? Let's think of all the things we might learn if Alice told us about her trip to the science museum." Answers are written on the blackboard, each answer praised with: "That's another thing we might learn," or "That's another idea!" No judgment is made about any child's offering.[9]

Verbal initiative is also enhanced when children are provided with fascinating stories or films. A story can be read up to a point of suspense, and each child can then be encouraged to tell his opinion of how the story might go on from there. Emphasis should be placed upon generating different ideas rather than guessing the "real" ending. A variation on this activity is to present the beginning and ending of a story and have the child create an exciting middle:

> George has just moved into a new town. He does not know anybody and feels lonely. The story ends with George having many good friends and feeling at home in the town. Begin the story with George in his room immediately after arriving in town, and end it when he has friends and feels at home.[10]

The teacher can make up these stories to fit the interest and age of the children in his class. Again, the idea is to involve the children in providing ideas and possibilities without consideration of what might be correct, and with no judgment made by the teacher of the value of any idea or solution.

Summary

The under-involved youngster does not enter into discussion, assume initiative, or seem to relate his personal or outside life to what is going on in the classroom. What he produces may or may not be "correct," but in either case it does not bear his personal stamp. His imagination, interests and feelings remain unconnected to classroom experience, and one does not enrich the other. The obvious consequence of this is a limited verbal interaction between him and others in the classroom and a decrease in his level of learning.

The techniques suggested in working with such a child include steps to involve parents more with both the child's schoolwork and with the school itself. Within school, curricula can intentionally be designed to highlight the relationship between classroom work and the child's experiences outside of school. It also becomes important for the teacher to take special steps to learn about the child's interests and skills, and to use this knowledge as a bridge relating the child to his classroom work. A further personal bridge must be established between the teacher and child to encourage him to "open up" and to share his interests and thoughts with others. Specific techniques can help the youngster enter step-by-step into dialogue with peers, and feel at ease in contributing ideas. Techniques which encourage verbalization also serve to pull the child into intellectual give-and-take.

The common goal of all the suggested techniques is to get the child to commit himself to what he is doing in the classroom. At times this cannot be rushed. The reticent child needs the active support of the teacher. Many uninvolved children do not enter personally into their work because they are afraid that judgment will be passed on them and their ideas. In fact, passive behavior is often perpetuated by adult judgmental attitudes or indifference to a child's ideas. To increase the child's involvement, a setting must be created that is not judgmental, that encourages the expression of ideas and opinions, and that takes joy in the new, the unusual, and the personal touch.

Footnotes

[1] E. Erikson. *Childhood and society.* New York: W. W. Norton and Co., 1963, p. 255.

[2] P. Mussen and C. Kuhlman. Initiating responses. In J. Bruner (Ed.), *Learning about learning.* USDHEW Cooperative Research Monograph No. 15, 1966, 14-21.

[3] M. S. Swift. Training poverty mothers in communication skills. *The Reading Teacher,* 1970, *23,* 360-367.

[4] E. P. Torrance and R. E. Myers. *Creative learning and teaching.* New York: Dodd, Mead and Co., 1971, pp. 138-144.

[5] P. Friedman. Relationship of teacher reinforcement to spontaneous student verbalization within the classroom. *Journal of Educational Psychology,* 1973, *65,* 59-64.

[6] Torrance and Myers, p. 261.

[7] Ibid., p. 90.

[8] E. P. Torrance and P. Torrance. Combining creative problem-solving with creative expression activities in the education of disadvantaged young people. *The Journal of Creative Behavior,* 1972, *6,* 1-10.

[9] G. Spivack and M. B. Shure. *Social adjustment of young children: A cognitive approach to solving real-life problems.* San Francisco: Jossey-Bass, 1974.

[10] M. B. Shure and G. Spivack. Means-ends thinking, adjustment and social class among elementary-school-aged children. *Journal of Consulting and Clinical Psychology,* 1972, *38,* 348-353.

7 Promoting Relevant Talk

The behaviors in this dimension involve a kind of talk and way of responding that is irrelevant to and often intrusive upon class discussions and activities. The youngster answers questions in class, but his answers often have nothing or little to do with the questions. He may grasp only a peripheral element, and then respond mainly in terms of an inner thought stimulated by that element, or even with an answer reflecting a personal preoccupation. He may interrupt when the teacher or another student is talking, as though prompted only by his need to say something and not whether the time or his comment is appropriate. Thus, such a youngster is eager to contribute to class discussions, but his comments may be irrelevant or peripheral, causing the discussion to wander off the point. Such a youngster may then talk about what is on his mind all day long if the teacher lets him. His stories frequently sound exaggerated or obviously untrue.

In more extreme instances, youngsters not only interrupt with irrelevant answers, but continually make wild guesses, forget what they have just said and lose their train of thought. The impulse to respond in terms of inner need rather than social or logical reasonableness may even reach the point (in extremely disturbed youngsters) where the child responds solely on the basis of his inner preoccupation, with total indifference to the reality of the class discussion.

Whatever the extent of these behaviors, however, there are always two related aspects at play. One aspect is impulsive verbal responding in ways which intrude on others' discussions or interrupt the flow of conversation. The behavior is not deliberately provocative or intended to disrupt. It reflects the child's inner pressure to verbalize his thoughts coupled with limited awareness of or concern for what is going on around him. The second aspect is the inappropriateness of the child's comments, which are generally personal or egocentric and reflect what the child has in mind; that is, his personal concern or interest, and not necessarily what others are discussing or wish to hear. Thus, his comments are not only intrusive and "unmannered" in style, but also irrelevant and unpredictable in content.

While such verbally intrusive responding is different from physical restlessness or impatience, each of these behaviors reveals to some extent a lack of thought-guided and thought-restrained action. Among emotionally disturbed children, irrelevant responsiveness is particularly evident in those who are also withdrawn and inattentive to what is going on in class. Thus, for some youngsters who display irrelevant talk it is useful to refer to Chapter 2, Increasing Attentiveness, Decreasing Withdrawal, when designing a teaching plan. In open classrooms, irrelevant talk is most apt to be displayed by the child who is too quick to respond in other ways, for instance, the child who starts work before getting the directions straight, and is unreflective about and impatient with work demands.[1] Strategies for aiding children with these difficulties are the focus of Chapter 5, Slowing Down the Impatient Child. Whether or not accompanied by these other qualities, however, irrelevant talk is not conducive to learning and requires stratagems of response on the part of the teacher in regular, open, or special classes.

Alternative Teaching Strategies

When planning teaching strategies for these youngsters, it is important to recognize that sometimes they call out answers, or respond with inappropriate answers because they are under pressure to be recognized by the teacher. They feel left out, and rush to participate in discussion without sufficient forethought to what they can contribute and how what they say may fit into what is going on in class. They feel unnoticed, want attention, and have not found an appropriate way of getting it. When such a child interrupts, calls out, or exaggerates in his stories, he is saying to the teacher: "I want you to listen to me, and it doesn't matter if you listen to what I'm saying or not, just listen to *me*!"

Because these intrusive and irrelevant comments tend to disrupt the child's learning they cannot simply be ignored. This is true even though speaking out of turn and interrupting can often be diminished by ignoring the child when he behaves in this manner. However, for such children merely ignoring their interrupting behaviors does not serve to promote relevant, reality-based thinking. When confronted with such behavior, the teacher must make an effort to listen carefully to what is being said. This will provide the child with the attention he may be seeking, and also allow the teacher to ascertain if it is necessary to help the child to distinguish external issues from fantasy or imagination. If added attention is all that is needed, the display of irrelevance, exaggerated stories and calling out may be decreased by arranging for brief private meetings if only for a few minutes a day, at which the child is encouraged to talk about what is on his mind. The teacher might also successfully alleviate the pressure for attention by reassuring the child in such simple ways as occasionally putting his arm on the youngster's shoulder, calling his name as they pass in the hallway, and talking to him in a personalized manner. Within the academic program the teacher can plan to directly include the child in a lesson. For example, during a spelling or language arts session the youngster's name can be used in a sentence or story.

In order to foster appropriate ways of responding, rather than shouting out, the teacher can indicate awareness of the youngster by calling on him when he does raise his hand or gives some other clue that he wishes to speak. As with so many other inappropriate behaviors, the teacher can strengthen the message to the child by verbalizing recognition of his self-control, in this case by stating how pleased he is that the youngster waited to be called upon rather than shouting out an answer. "You were very patient and waited until I could call on you. I'm pleased. And now you know that I will be calling on you when you want to talk." Such attention and guidance does not "baby" the youngster, and there is no reason to fear he will need such attention indefinitely. Giving attention to this child without hesitation whenever he draws attention to himself by making a relevant response may make long-range plans for overcoming irrelevance and interrupting unnecessary.

For many youngsters, however, it is often necessary to use additional approaches in order to aid their classroom performance. Teaching techniques that foster the child's ability to respond both with relevant content and in a relevant manner involve (1) clarifying social rules and external demands; (2) educating reflectiveness; (3) helping the child, and the teacher, think about and relate answers and ideas to topics being considered; and (4) helping the youngster define and distinguish between reality and fantasy. None of these techniques is more appropriate than any other; in many instances a combination of these techniques is the most valuable.

Clarifying social
rules and external demands

More often than not impulsive and inappropriate responding reflects more than a strong need for attention. One element is an apparent difficulty in restraining verbal reaction. For this youngster, something thought is something said. He has not developed the skill of holding back a thought while someone else is talking, nor does he have a sufficient counterbalancing appreciation of another person's ideas or need to express them. Listening demands too much concentration upon external events and too much waiting before expressing one's own ideas.

Since learning requires concentrated attention to what is going on, plus the willingness to attempt to interchange ideas following such attention, one useful approach requires that the teacher clearly spell out the reasons why everyone cannot speak out whenever he wants. While not moralizing, it is appropriate to discuss the issue of "good manners." Although many teachers tell the child, "It is good manners to listen to others and to wait your turn," this is rarely enough to change the child's behavior. It is helpful to follow such a comment by discussing with the youngster why it is necessary to listen and wait, encouraging him to express his thoughts about why this is so important. The teacher might explain that interrupting another person hurts feelings, that when someone shouts out no one else may want to listen to him, and that when he interrupts others they may get angry and not want to be his friends. There are many consequences of interrupting and those emphasized by the teacher may be geared to the particular child's personality. The gregarious child would not want to feel that he might lose friends. The child who values the teacher highly may not like the prospect of hurting his feelings or alienating his affections. A youngster with a deep sense of "fairness" would not want to feel that he is considered unfair by his peers. If more than one or two youngsters tend to respond this way, these issues may be taken up in a discussion with the class as a whole.

These youngsters are often unaware of what they are doing or do not appreciate the effect their behavior has upon others. They may receive negative reactions from classmates, but may view such reactions as unjust, without understanding that what they do produces these reactions. Classroom discussion, as long as it is not a personal attack on anyone, can open up these issues and afford the child a new appreciation of what is at stake. The fact that one or two students need such help may even be mentioned, as long as the teacher creates a setting wherein the question is how the class can help the particular students with their "overenthusiasm."

Such a class discussion may be introduced by the teacher with the statement: "Whenever people get together and talk, they follow certain rules—they listen to others, they wait for another person to finish talking before they start." The teacher might then pose such questions as: "Why do you think people act this way? What are social manners? How do they help us to learn? What happens when we are trying to talk or ask a question and someone interrupts?" Everyone should be encouraged to offer reasons and explanations. To provide guidelines, the teacher can suggest that each child think about whether he is sticking to the point and is listening to the points others are making. "Are you showing that you are concerned about the other people in the class? How are you doing it?" Reasons why some people do not obey social rules may be explored, as well as what can best be done when someone loses track of the social situation. Specific solutions may be sought which can help all the students to show consideration for the ideas of others. Such issues as "consideration," "interrupting" and "sticking to the point" should be carefully defined so that the child who is not responding in a relevant way can be brought back into the discussion by reminding him to think about these concepts.

It is also helpful, in private talks with such a youngster, to get his views on what he and the teacher might do to help matters. If he is unaware of when he is getting away from the topic and thereby interrupting the thinking of others, a cue may be worked out through which the teacher can let him know when he has interrupted, or is in the process of doing so. Such an approach has been called "signal interference"[2] and is amplified in Chapter 10, Meeting the Needs of the Restless, Socially Overinvolved Student.

Educating reflectiveness

It is often necessary for the teacher to go beyond discussion of social rules and to plan a specific training approach to decrease a child's "impulsive tempo."[3] As a first step the teacher may respond to the child in a way which indicates that they have similar interests and things in common to talk about. The teacher may question the child about his family, favorite foods, games and animals, responding with pleasure and pointing out "how many things we have in common—we both like (oranges, movies, etc.). We are the same!" This "similarity training" is aimed at helping the child see himself as more like the teacher and can be built upon for the second step, that of encouraging the child to follow the teacher's example of how to think before saying what is on his mind.

Following this effort to establish a bond based upon similarity of interests, the child should be provided with training in taking his time and thinking before giving his answer to a problem. The teacher can say:

> We're so much the same on so many things that I'm going to tell you something about myself. Maybe we can be the same on that, too. I think it's important not to make mistakes and to be right. So I take my time and always check my answers. One of the things we're going to do together is some. . . games. . . . The important thing in these games is to try not to make a mistake. I want you to get them right every time on your first try and one way to get them right is to think about your answer.[4]

Following this explanation the teacher can demonstrate how he pauses before answering an academic problem, emphasizing that when he is uncertain he thinks about what to say before saying it. The child can then be instructed that he is not allowed to give any answer to a problem until he waits for 10 to 15 seconds, thus requiring the child to study the problem and to think about what he is going to say.[5]

Fostering the relationship between the teacher and child (see Chapter 4) is an effective and important means for increasing a variety of behaviors conducive to learning.

Knowledge of this method of getting the child to relate to and identify with the teacher may be valuable whenever a technique calls for the child to follow the lead of the teacher.

Relating answers to questions

The youngster who responds with irrelevant talk may also need training in relating answers to questions. His answers may often bear no relationship to what has been asked, even after training to think before answering. His answers also appear to be incorrect or even egocentric, touched off by his own inner associations rather than the questions.

It is important for the teacher to look beyond what a child says by questioning a response which seems irrelevant or is different from expectations. When teaching young children to think of their own solutions to real-life interpersonal problems, children sometimes give answers that *seem* inappropriate or irrelevant:

> In response to how a boy playing ball with another boy might feel, most children agreed that he was probably feeling happy. One child said, "He is sad." At first the teacher thought the child still did not understand the difference between happy and sad. Instead of correcting him, however, the teacher asked him why he thought the boy might be sad. The child replied, "The ball might hit him in the eye." In response to a problem dealing with how a boy can get a fireman to give him a ride on the firetruck, a child said, "Look in his mommy's pocketbook." When asked how that could get him a ride, he answered, "Then he can give him the money."[6]

A similar episode occurred when a teacher asked a girl to "tell two factors which contributed toward the development of the city (of Chicago)." The child's reply was, "The lake and the cow that kicked the bucket and started the big fire." This was met with puzzlement. The teacher asked, "And what has the cow to do with it?" And the child replied, "Well, after the city burned down, they had to build it up again, and they made it bigger and nicer." Apparently viewing this as inappropriate, the teacher turned to another student without replying to the first child, thus missing an opportunity to encourage the child for her effort and thinking. Teachers who insist upon only a predetermined correct answer

> . . . are dull teachers, responsible not only for the boredom of their students, but for many discipline problems that come up because of a rigid, stale, and antiquated method of teaching. It is not uncommon to find children who, because of such teaching, decide that they don't like social studies or arithmetic, and so on.[7]

A more effective way to handle such a response is for the teacher to indicate to the child that he had not thought of that answer but recognizes the connection that the child made as well as the fact that the child is attempting to reply in a relevant manner.

Thus, when the student responds in what appears to be an irrelevant manner, as a first step the teacher might explore with him the relationship the student sees between his answer and the question. If the effort is to draw the child into relevant classroom activities and discussion, then as a standard procedure the teacher might reply, "That is a very interesting idea. Can you think of another way to answer that question?" The child is more apt to learn if the teacher is open to unique interpretations and ideas, and makes an effort to help the child increase his ability to relate them to questions. "I'm not sure I understand, Ted, but I'd like to know more about your answer. Could you explain to me what you meant when you answered the question I asked?" Having the student explain may reveal the connection he saw or, as noted above, indicate an appropriate thought worth pursuing further. To help the youngster make the connection between a question and his answers, it is important to learn about the youngster's view of the question.

If a discussion reveals that the child's response does not reflect an awareness of what was asked, the teacher may repeat the question and ask the youngster to think about what it means before trying to answer. The youngster should be instructed, "Give an answer that will make it possible for others to understand what you are trying to tell them about the question." This strategy helps the youngster to focus on the question by fostering an awareness of the importance of his answers to communication and interaction. When the student focuses on the question as well as the answer, his reply will usually become relevant, or he will say that he does not know the answer. In the latter instance the teacher can reply, "That's OK, Ted. It's all right if you don't know the answer as long as you know the question. So think about it some more. You do not have to give just any answer. The important thing is to give the answer that fits the question. We can find out what it is together. Let's see if someone else has any thoughts about how to answer this question."

Another way to emphasize the importance of the question is to have the youngster repeat it himself even before trying to grapple with it, and have him restate it after a while for the rest of the group. The youngster prone to respond to questions in an irrelevant manner may be given the job of "keeper of the question" who from time to time is the only one told the question. His job is to relay that question to others in the class at the beginning of a discussion, as well as to repeat it periodically. By returning to the question for restatement during a discussion, its importance becomes the focus of the child's attention. Furthermore, having the child restate a question in his own words increases his involvement with and commitment to the problem.[8]

Group games can be helpful in training attention to the continuity of thoughts stimulated by a question posed in class. A group may be asked to create a "chain" story from a question, such as: "What happened when Jack sold the cow for magic beans?" One child then continues to tell the story where a previous youngster left off. Here the effort is to highlight how one person's thoughts are related to another's. This game demands that each child attend to the flow of talk because he may be called upon to answer the question, "What happens next?"

Another useful approach is one in which someone suggests a topic and then enlists the group in asking and answering questions about it. For example, the topic suggested might be "A trip to Puerto Rico." Each youngster is asked to think of a question about the trip. Each question is written on the blackboard and then referred to: "Now, what might be an answer to this question?" Each answer is recorded and the group is asked to decide which answers show that the person was thinking about the question and why. This procedure gives the group and the teacher the opportunity to highlight the essentials of each question, and how the answers relate to each question: "Yes, what to wear is important. The people in Puerto Rico probably don't wear fur coats in the winter like we do because Puerto Rico is nearer to the equator than we are. The nearer the equator the hotter the temperature, even in the winter."

If a student has given an irrelevant answer but can change it with little prompting from the class or the teacher, it may only be necessary to comment: "Oh, now we see what you meant. You really cleared that up for us. It helped us to learn when you made your answer fit the question." In other situations, the teacher might respond to an answer which has nothing to do with the question by saying: "Remember how you (or another youngster) cleared up your (his) answer to the question about. . . ? It helped us to understand when you made your answer fit the question. Can you make your answer fit this question?" As noted earlier, the teacher might repeat the question and indicate to the child that he should think about how he can give an answer for this question. "You think about it and when you are ready, raise your hand and I'll call on you." If there is some doubt about the child's understanding of the question he might be asked to explain it to the teacher. In order to be sure that the answer he gives in front of the group is relevant, the teacher might ask the child to "tell me first and we'll talk about your answer."

All of the above teaching techniques are designed to make the child more aware that there are relevant and irrelevant ways of dealing with questions, and that others expect him to give answers that fit the question. If the teacher does not develop methods to foster this behavior and allows irrelevant answers to pass, the youngster will become confused. He senses from the reaction of the teacher and the class that something is wrong, but does not know for sure what is wrong or how to correct it.

When a youngster is unable to clarify his thoughts in response to questions, it may be necessary to work more specifically with him to identify what is really true and what he just thinks is true. As extreme as this may seem, studies indicate that a sizeable proportion of elementary school children, even those of normal intelligence in regular classes, are unclear about the difference between what they think and what is really true, much like the younger, preschool child. Some intervention is needed if they are to learn to respond in a manner conducive to academic success.

Distinguishing
between reality and fantasy

Some youngsters not only fail to relate their thoughts to questions, but may also exaggerate when telling about events. In such instances, the youngster responds to what is going on in class with irrelevant, "personal" thoughts which are difficult for others to relate to the flow of classroom discussion. He does not make appropriate distinctions between what "is," what might or might not be true, and what is shared knowledge vs. his own personal view of things. While it is unwise to discourage creative imagination, it is also necessary to help such children establish for themselves some notion of "reality" (or shared consensus of opinion and fact), what is possibly true, what is probably not true, and what could never be true (in all likelihood). It is important for him to learn that there is a difference between fantasy and socially agreed-upon facts, and that both have their place in the classroom.

In the group situation, the teacher may use storytelling as a vehicle for questioning about these matters: "Do you think what Huckleberry Finn said was true, or just made up?" "Why do you think so, Jimmy?" Statements may be made up by the teacher that mix reality, exaggeration, and pure fantasy or unlikely occurrences. The teacher can read these statements and ask the class to find which parts of them were probably possible, which were somewhat exaggerated, and which were not true. For example: "The astronaut ran up the stairs to get into the nose of the rocket. It was a two-mile long rocket. He was a little nervous. He was well trained for his flight. He got tired of running up the stairs so he took the elevator. He knew it would take him a long time to get to the sun, but he was anxious to begin his long voyage to meet the people who lived on this planet. They started the countdown: 10, 9, 8, 11, 19, 27, 6, 5, 4, 3, 10. . . and finally the rocket rose off the launch pad." Each element in such stories can be questioned for its credibility— what could be true, what definitely is true, and what definitely is not. Youngsters involved in discussions of such stories may argue about evidence, but the goal is to make it clear that some things are true and some things are exaggerations or just not so. Distinctions between fact and opinion may be highlighted, as well as distinctions between consensually shared facts and one's private fantasy.

The teacher may also wish to pursue such distinctions with the youngster in individual assignments. For example, the youngster may be asked to write a short, true story about a dog, "a story that really happened." When he is done, he can then be asked to write a story about the same dog but one that is unlikely, though possible, "a story that could happen but didn't." Finally, he may be asked to write a story that is clearly impossible, "a make-believe or pretend story, one you made up just for fun, but can't happen." At each stage, the teacher can engage the youngster in discussion about how the stories are different.

Without such planned approaches it is easy for a teacher to fall into the role of prosecuting attorney, attempting to pin down a youngster about an exaggeration, or the "truth" of something he has asserted. Such a confrontation must be avoided. The intention is to draw the youngster into the class activities, not cause him to pull away. If he asserts something is true that is rather hard to believe, it may be necessary to point out that his statement is difficult to believe, or to raise the possibility of a slight exaggeration. The teacher might ask, "Is that a story like the ones we were making up the other day about the dog?" If the youngster challenges the teacher with a statement such as: "But it did happen. Don't you believe me?" then the best response is to tell him that all a teacher can do is listen carefully to what is said and ask about everyone's interesting ideas. If the child has a sense of humor, or is somewhat aware of what he is doing, the teacher might say: "Yes, I always take what you say seriously, but sometimes you do tell a good story!" Whenever the teacher judges that a youngster is exaggerating, perhaps without realizing he has slipped into it, it is a good technique to talk with him after class about his opinions: "Is what you said today really true, do you think, or was part of it a story?" "It is good to make up interesting stories; was what you said today a good story, or did it really happen?" If the youngster insists that what he said is true, it is not wise to challenge him about it. The teacher has made the point that the distinction is important, that he values both fact and fancy, but that he believes everyone should keep in mind the difference. The important issue here is not to establish if the child has lied, but to help him to distinguish fact from imagination.

Legitimizing fantasy

In eagerness to assist a youngster to clarify his views about what is real and what is fantasy, teachers should not succumb to the notion that fantasy is bad, or fail to recognize that an atmosphere which is conducive to the free use of imagination can also be conducive to problem-solving and academic growth. Youngsters who display irrelevant talk often have an active imagination that exerts a pressure for expression, and that can be capitalized on to foster productive performance. Their style of thinking about the world is often quite expressive and more open than most. Thus, what is a problem can become an asset.

Although it is more difficult for this child than for others to maintain a purely controlled and rational response to life, he may have less trouble and become less troublesome when given an opportunity to express his fantasy or imagination in a socially acceptable form. If old enough to write, he may be asked to write down his ideas about a current class issue, or put these ideas into a story. The teacher can actively encourage this form of expression whenever possible, and regard the product as a "made-up story" through which to help the child develop his expressive style. If fantasy is to be drawn out, it is best to ignore such issues as spelling and grammar. For the youngster too young to write, the teacher may write down the story or teach him to use a tape recorder. The issue is to provide experiences which show that the teacher supports the expression of fantasy, but at the same time build up a clear demarcation between fiction and fact. Enthusiasm can be shown for how imaginative an idea is, identifying it as the child's "mystery" or "adventure" story and enjoying it with him.

Summary

Irrelevant responding may reflect a number of problems. The child may (1) be unaware of social protocol, (2) not know how to restrain the first impulse to answer, (3) need help in relating ideas to a class topic, or (4) need to learn to distinguish fact from personal imagining.

Interrupting and failing to stay with the point of a discussion often indicates a youngster does not understand how to interact smoothly with others in situations where the give and take of ideas is appropriate. Although desirous of contact with others and alert to what is going on, the youngster may fail to act as a contributing member because of a poorly developed sense of social rules and the rights of others. The child may need to learn that others have feelings and wish to contribute ideas, and that to get along in social situations he must listen to others and has the right to expect them to listen to him. If a child acts pressured to talk and interrupt, even though he knows it is wrong, it may be useful to emphasize that he deserves the attention of the class when he has something to say, and so need not hurry to get it out.

Often these students need to learn specific ways to delay responding before talking. The teacher can use his own behavior as a model of reflectiveness, and as such can aid the student by demonstrating how to go about thinking before making a response. This child also needs to learn that the answer, in itself, is not the only thing to talk about, but that an answer is good because it relates to the question. Teachers are cautioned that if the concern is only with gaining a pre-determined answer, then the child who responds with any-thing else will appear to be providing irrelevant information. Further exploration of a child's seemingly irrelevant com-ments can open the teacher's eyes to the child's ideas as well as provide opportunities to encourage relevant involvement and thinking. A final goal in working with this child is that he learn to differentiate between what is thought or imagined and what is true. The child must learn that his imagination is part of him and is valued, but he must also be able to tell a story or exaggerate and recognize it as such.

It is important to realize that the underlying tone of the child's responses usually reflects a desire for involvement and communication of personal thought (albeit irrelevant) and not an intent to fabricate, disrupt or reject what is going on in class.

Footnotes

[1] G. Spivack and M. Swift. Behavioral adjustment in the open classroom. *International Journal of Applied Psychology*, in press.

[2] R. Redl and D. Wineman. *Controls from within*. Glencoe: The Free Press, 1952, pp. 160-163.

[3] J. Kagan, L. Pearson and L. Welch. Modifiability of an impulsive tempo. *Journal of Educational Psychology*, 1966, *57*, 359-365.

[4] Ibid., p. 361.

[5] Ibid.

[6] G. Spivack and M. Shure. *Social adjustment of young children: A cognitive approach to solving real-life problems*. San Francisco: Jossey-Bass, 1974, p. 34.

[7] R. Dreikurs, D. B. Grunwald and F. C. Pepper. *Maintaining sanity in the classroom*. New York: Harper and Row, 1971, p. 176.

[8] M. Henle. Cognitive skills. In J. Bruner (Ed.), *Learning about learning*. USDHEW Cooperative Research Monograph No. 15, 1966.

8 Coping with Negative Feelings and Actions

The behavior dimensions discussed in other chapters, such as restlessness, blaming, impatience, interrupting or inattentiveness, may at times tax the teacher's patience or appear to challenge the teacher's leadership role. However, none of these dimensions has directly implicated a student's negative motivation, defiance or disobedience.

The present dimension subsumes such negative and at times aggressively "disobedient" behaviors. The youngster may speak in a manner which suggests a lack of respect for the teacher: he may call the teacher names, or in other ways attempt to diminish the teacher's esteem. He may also respond with defiance, refusing to do what is asked of him, such as following the teacher's directions.

This open rebellion may take the form of criticizing the academic subject matter ("Spelling is stupid") or belittling the importance or interest value of classroom activities ("This is all silly"; "Who has to know this?" "I have more important ways to spend my time"). The youngster may vent his defiance by breaking rules. He may throw things, mark up or tear pages of books, mar desks, and in variety of ways damage classroom equipment. Some youngsters may be more subtle, for example, claiming that the teacher did not say or request something that the teacher in fact did, or criticizing the school and teacher within earshot of the teacher.

Older youngsters may criticize their peers as well. Another student's opinion may be criticized in a negative way, or his work may be called foolish or senseless. When a fellow student asks a question, the question may be called stupid or in other ways belittled, and an attempt may be made to make the other student the brunt of peer laughter and ridicule.

The common element in all of these behaviors is the tendency to diminish the significance of the entire educational enterprise, with the intent to eliminate the credibility of everyone associated with it. In extreme instances such attempts to belittle and undermine go beyond the teacher and the subject matter, and extend to other students trying to perform well. Their performance gives legitimacy to the entire enterprise, and so they also must be ridiculed.

The blatant expression of negative feelings and disobedient behavior is more likely to occur in special classes for behaviorally or emotionally disturbed youngsters. In part, this reflects the fact that many children are assigned to such classes only after long-term failure on their parts, failure compounded by associated kinds of disruptive and negative behaviors which bring them to the attention of school counselors and psychologists. Furthermore, these problem behaviors are more likely to occur in the special class setting where teachers are more apt to try to understand and work with the expression of negative feelings and actions. However, they do occur in all schools and in each instance reflect some level of alienation from the classroom enterprise. Wherever it appears, this alienation indicates serious trouble and lack of achievement, thus demanding carefully planned intervention approaches.

Before leaving the discussion of aggressively negative and disobedient behaviors, it is important to point out what behaviors do *not* reflect this dimension, even though they may appear openly defiant on the surface. Some children will argue with the teacher, even though it is fairly obvious to the teacher that the student may have insufficient information to challenge his knowledge and experience. Other youngsters will openly challenge what the teacher says, asserting that they have information inconsistent with what the teacher has said. It is easy to get into detailed and entangling discussions with such youngsters, some of whom seem to take delight in amassing facts and demonstrating their proficiency. Some youngsters will quibble with the teacher or try to prove that a test answer is right when it was scored as "wrong." At times youngsters assert that the teacher said something the previous week different from what he is now saying, as though to catch him in an inconsistency.

Such behaviors may easily be misconstrued as having defiant or hostile intent when in fact they may not. Unlike the more defiant and negative behaviors, such challenging behaviors do not relate consistently to academic achievement. They do not imply a resistance to learning or disrespect for the teacher and classroom activities. They may mistakenly be interpreted as negative in intent because they *appear* to challenge the teacher's intellectual authority, and thus *seem* to have as their goal diminishing the teacher's self-respect. However, these behaviors usually reflect a stage in growth where the youngster has a need to assert some intellectual independence. He wants to feel that he can think for himself, and puts much of his own pride into intellectual mastery. His behavior is not directed *against* the teacher, but is a buttress for his own evolving sense of academic and intellectual competence. He is saying: "I am not a mere sponge, an absorber of information. I have a mind of my own and can think for myself. I will listen to what you are saying, but don't expect me to believe it all just because you say it. I will check it out for myself and come to my own opinions." He does not defiantly shut out the teacher and the learning process, but demands that he be the final judge of what he is to believe. He is not a passive learner or a classroom conformist. Hostility and negativism will only occur when the teacher's acts squelch his growth into assertive intellectual independence.

Returning to the current dimension of negative and disobedient behaviors, it is understood that all children may manifest some of these behaviors at times. However, a consistent pattern of such behaviors, even in moderate amounts, indicates that the youngster is being turned off, and is openly expressing his frustration and resentment. Excessive amounts of such behavior indicate that the youngster is alienated from the present learning environment and cannot benefit from what is happening in the classroom. Even worse, the problem is usually compounded because the classroom cannot contain him, and administrative action and labeling as a "special" student may follow. Too often this means the educational system has given up, and the youngster is doomed to educational deprivation.

Alternative Teaching Strategies

The child who is defiant with teachers and verbally negative toward peers, subject matter, and the school frequently prompts emotion-laden and angry responses from others. It is easy to understand how a teacher might become locked in a struggle of wills and power with a student who vents his angry feelings on the teacher. Maintaining composure is difficult when confronted with a child who acts as if he has no concern for the values and feelings of others. Even an excellent and usually very composed, successful teacher indicated that with one such child he "could have run him over with a car for the way he upset me." In the extreme, the behaviors go beyond breaking classroom rules, to the point where most of the generally accepted social standards appear to have little or no meaning. Alienation becomes so great that without alternatives to change the nature of their interactions, neither the student nor the teacher appears to see any hope for a relationship.

A plan for prevention and intervention *must* be instituted if the youngster is to remain in the classroom and eventually to gain from the school experience. It becomes necessary to develop ways to overcome disrupted relations particularly when the behavior advances to the emotion-provoking stage revealed by the teacher above.

Specific teaching strategies of most value in working with these children provide (1) structure and clarity about what is expected; (2) means of creating and maintaining an interpersonal bridge between teacher and child; (3) opportunities to air feelings about school demands; (4) activities to aid the learning of alternative ways of thinking and behaving; and (5) ways of heading off loss of control and handling emotional pressures.

Spelling out the rules and defining limits

A preventive plan of action is the best approach. It is necessary to establish, and establish early, a means whereby the child can learn and understand "rules to live by." The teacher should not assume that all youngsters understand what the expected standards are when they are breaking "the rules of the game"; they may also be unaware of the consequences of their own behavior.

When establishing limits, the intention is not to make a pronouncement or listing of rules on the first day of school. But, when working with a child whose behaviors will cause him continued failure in both academic and interpersonal spheres, the teacher must establish for the child's own sake what he can say and do and what is "out of bounds." The teacher must make clear that some behaviors are not acceptable because they impede learning and successful relationships, hurt the feelings of others, and probably under the best of circumstances bring negative consequences. These can be spelled out concretely by giving examples of unacceptable behavior such as: calling the teacher names, throwing things, tearing or marking books, saying "This is stupid," refusing to work, and telling other children that they are stupid. These behaviors must be discussed in words the student understands. It is of little avail to say to the child: "You are defiant. Your behavior is ugly."

It is also best if the teacher and student can together come to conclusions about living within these rules. Such students should be encouraged and helped to think about and discuss how they want to handle things they do not like, things that are important to learning and to relations with others. The teacher should indicate that a range of choices is available to anyone who wants to handle an activity differently from everyone else, and that no one has to feel that he must defy anyone to solve a problem. The teacher might pose the question: "What ways can a student show that he does not like something, besides saying, 'It's stupid?' Can you think of some other way you can tell how you feel about the rules? What other good ways are there to tell someone you don't like what they are doing? What might happen if you told me you did not like spelling? What do you think I could do that might help?" The goal of such discussions is to encourage the student to describe alternative ways of behaving and the consequences for each, and to indicate to him that there are effective ways of dealing with and questioning rules.

As part of the process of establishing basic rules and exploring them rationally the teacher must indicate that, "It is all right to do something your own way. I'll even help you do it. But you must do some work. If you don't do any work, or you continue to throw things or belittle others, it will lead to the consequences we have talked about."

Another approach is for the teacher to discuss with a student the consistency and appropriateness of the limits established. One of the problems for many seemingly defiant children is that most adults have been unclear about expectations, arbitrary in establishing rules, and inconsistent in dealing with inappropriate behaviors. For these reasons if rules have been set up for an entire class (e.g., anyone can go to the water fountain whenever a class lesson is not going on and when no one else is out of the room), then the teacher is bound by these rules for *all* children. The defiant child should be encouraged to keep his end of the agreement to follow these established rules, and the teacher must enforce these rules with equity.

Another facet of specifying rules of conduct directly involves the teacher, who should consider making a commitment to the child that he will not embarrass the child by calling attention to his defiant behavior in front of others. Keeping the issue between student and teacher a private matter not only helps to avoid new reasons for defiance (e.g., defense of pride), but also communicates to the child the teacher's genuine and personal commitment to work with him. The teacher must, at all costs, avoid doing anything that might suggest that he is taking vindictive action *against* the youngster. He must not hold a grudge, or let it be known that he is just "waiting for him to act up." By word and deed the child should be shown that reasonable and humane rules apply to the behavior of teachers as well as students. It must be made clear to the youngster that the teacher is bound by the same commitment to children that the children are being asked to show toward others. If an established rule is that each child is to get recess or a treat, or a chance to read, then every child, regardless of his behavior, must get his due. The youngster must not lose what is "due" him because he has misbehaved; rather, he (as well as any other student) might receive an extra treat if he has behaved appropriately or according to the rules.

One way to show that the teacher is willing to "give," while holding to certain rules, is to indicate that the youngster has some choice in how to do what the teacher requests. For example, if the youngster balks at doing math at 9 a.m., the teacher might say, "OK, here are the choices you have; out of these pick what you think is best." If the teacher wishes to remain firm about the math assignment, then the youngster may be told, "You don't have to do the math now, but it must be done by the end of the day." The idea is to provide acceptable alternatives to the ultimate conflict that this child continually brings on himself. It is useful to give the child leeway within the structured "rules of the game," leeway in which he does not feel forced to conform completely to the details or means of carrying out a task. As one teacher noted: "Having a face-to-face conflict is the worst thing you can do. Let him go, and ignore some of the behavior while indicating that you are maintaining your expectations. When he says, 'I'm not going to do it,' say, 'OK for now, you can do it later.' Let him exercise some choice. Don't make it a 'now or never' situation."

Establishing personal contact

To be sure that class discussion about rules for everyone has meaning to these children, the teacher must immediately follow up with personal contact or small group meetings to clarify what has been said. It is not wise to wait until after an act of defiance, and then say: "That's it. You defied me. That's something I didn't tell you about, but I don't like it. You're out." With some youngsters it is necessary to frequently repeat such discussions early in the year before disrupted relations become entrenched. Having had such contacts, the teacher is then able to respond to negative behaviors by restating the rules that "we" (teacher and child) set up. Repetition of personal contact is important, and a clear restatement of limits must be part of general class policy. Within these individual sessions it is imperative that the teacher communicate that it is the youngster's behavior that creates problems, but that he is still liked as a person. In this manner it is possible to establish early in the year and reestablish consistently thereafter that the teacher accepts the youngster, but not the behaviors which break *our* rules.

In general, as one teacher noted: "It is most important to realize that the negative child has many unhappy feelings about school and himself. Don't belittle, criticize, call him names, or display anger. Approach him as an individual with his own set of needs, desires, capabilities; capitalize on his interests. Most importantly, let him know that he has as much status as everyone else, including all the teachers."

Looking for and responding to positive behaviors of children who are "defiant" and "disrespectful" is often difficult because of the unhappy feelings such youngsters generate in their teachers. Another difficulty is that these youngsters often actively rebuff adult attempts to be close to them, in large part because they do not believe any adult can honestly want to know or to like them. For this reason the teacher cannot assume that he has made a point of showing special interest after only one or two tries. He must not give up because his first efforts are rejected by the youngster. Part of the frustration in establishing a relationship with such a child stems from the child's history of failures and negative feelings about adults. To overcome this, the teacher must make efforts to establish a bond and maintain it over time as well as continually during the school day.

In spite of the relative frequency of a child's defiant behavior, the teacher must always seek times to talk to him when he is not acting this way, saying, "You're such a good boy when you. . ." or "I like the work you did this morning." The teacher should not be tempted to say, "Why can't you be that way all the time?" In fact, *as often as is feasible,* the negative behavior should be ignored, but in order for the impact of ignoring inappropriate behavior to be felt it is necessary that the teacher deliberately look for times to respond positively when the student is *not* defiant. As the teacher walks around the classroom or in the halls after class, he should consider going a little out of his way to talk with the child again, to joke or have a small aside with him, particularly when he is behaving appropriately.

Overcoming crises

In a "crisis" situation where it is essential that the teacher respond with some action, it is often best to remove this child from the classroom *before* talking to him. Peer pressure may provoke more defiant behavior if the child is singled out for verbal interchange in class. He may feel compelled to defy even a teacher he likes because his peers are listening. In short, things can only become worse when confrontation is direct and in front of other children.

Whether during crises or calm times, personal discussion between teacher and child should not focus solely upon problem incidents. If possible, the teacher should seek out the child to discuss a positive thing he has done, activities he obviously enjoys or does well, or some aspects of their relationship. This requires looking beyond the crisis episode to indicate that all is not lost and that the teacher is willing to reach out in a variety of ways to establish a relationship. The teacher might comment about how pleased he is that the youngster helped another child or seemed to have fun during a particular activity. A common ground for discussion might be established around the teacher's value of the student and his interests. One useful approach for laying the groundwork for a relationship with such youngsters is to say to the student at a time of subdued behavior: "Gosh, Paul, if I couldn't sit down and talk to you I would be disappointed. You seem to understand me when we talk like this. You know some of the things I am talking about. When we talk like this, Paul, I feel like I understand you and you listen to me. I like it best when we work things out like this rather than arguing about them."

In this way the teacher states in the simplest terms that a positive relationship is possible and is desired. The youngster's name should be interjected several times during these pleasant discussions. Many such youngsters become used to hearing their names only when a teacher is reprimanding them for misbehavior. This approach communicates to the youngster his importance in the eyes of the teacher, and that the teacher is willing to spend time with him in pleasant discussion, and not just when a crisis arises.

Airing dissent and questioning school

Beyond the clarification of appropriate and inappropriate behaviors, it is useful to hold discussions around: "Why do we learn to read? What good is reading (spelling, etc.)?" The teacher may raise questions about why anyone would come to school, and encourage dissenting opinions. Some children will say they come to school to learn, others will say because "my mother makes me come." Both are legitimate reasons and should be acknowledged as such. Acceptance of feelings is one major step in the process of drawing a defiant child toward the teacher, as someone who wants to and can understand him.

Thus, it is important for the teacher to recognize the need to express certain negative feelings and attitudes toward school, peers, subject matter and teacher. These students should be encouraged to question the work requirements and to draw their own conclusions about the "need" to go to school or to learn to read. It may seem that allowing such questioning is counter to the notion that everyone "must" do some work, as established during discussion of classroom rules. However, establishing rules is only one step in the process of involving defiant children in the learning process. In the long run, these students must see that some of their questions and criticisms are legitimate and that the teacher is able to understand and accept their negative feelings, comments, and behaviors without turning against them as people.

Providing alternatives

Because the teacher must help the child to keep his defiance from getting out of hand, *without* calling attention directly to the defiance, it is helpful if diversions are planned which enable the youngster to move away from an activity that causes defiance. If defiant behavior occurs in a particular context or during a particular activity, the teacher can avoid confrontation with the youngster by letting him know that he can engage in another, less provoking activity. The teacher can then return the child to the original activity only for brief periods of time after the diversion has calmed the situation.

Such diversions may be carried out in a number of ways. One approach to the student who refuses to sit in his seat when all others are asked to do so might be to have him hand out books and papers. It is important to divert the child before the defiant behavior becomes entrenched. Thus, if a child says, "No I won't," the teacher can decide if his response to the child should be "Yes you will" or "Come here, I have a job for you. Please hand out these papers."

The teacher may also divert a student's refusal to do work or negative comments about subject matter by saying: "Yes, sometimes we do feel that spelling is stupid and don't want to do it. Some of the other children need to study spelling words. If you don't want to study your words, why don't you go over and work with (name another child who is in need of help and is at a lower level) and help him with his words?"

Another approach involves recognition of something "clever" about what the child is doing, telling him so, and then asking him to think of some other (more productive) activity that he can do with the teacher or his peers. For example, a child tied a rope to the classroom door from the playground and was opening the door by pulling on the rope. Rather than risking a negative, defiant reply to a request to untie the rope, the teacher asked the child what he was doing and he answered, "Opening the door." The teacher then stated, "What a clever idea to use the rope to pull the door open," and smiled at the child. "Can you think of some other clever place to tie the rope?" The child stopped for a minute, untied the rope and took it to the outer fence of the schoolyard where he retied the rope. The teacher then called some other children to play jump the rope.

Playing good behavior games. "Good behavior games" are designed to enlist an entire class in aiding one or a few of the class members.

One such game has been designed to present students with appropriate behaviors to frustration-inducing situations likely to lead to aggressive behavior. The effort is to increase the number of alternative responses verbalized by the students when confronted with such a situation. An example of a frustrating classroom situation used in the game is: "You're ready for your teacher to check your workbook, and he keeps helping another child with a very simple problem." Prior to playing the game the children can be taught and given a chance to practice five responses of appropriate behavior to each frustrating situation in the game.

The game is played like most commercially available table games with a path to move around by counting the total on a rolled pair of dice. Each play begins at a common starting point and the player follows directions on the space where he lands. Some of the spaces on the board allow the player to pick an "appropriate behavior response card" which he keeps until he lands on a space describing one of a number of real-life, frustrating situations the teacher has made up. If the player has the right "appropriate behavior response card" for that frustrating situation, he can draw another card for a surprise. The surprise cards are worth different amounts of points. At the end of the game surprise card points are added and bonuses awarded for each set of five appropriate behavior response cards held.

By playing this game, the child learns correct responses which he must know before he can be expected to act correctly. However, if he is to continue the desired behaviors, it is necessary to follow correct behavior with a reinforcing activity that is pleasurable or reward the child in some way. This type of good behavior game encourages the child to talk about frustrating situations, provides him with alternative appropriate behaviors, and in turn, presents the teacher with opportunities to respond to the child's positive behaviors with approval and praise.[1]

Another type of game centers around a good behavior clock which indicates when the student is, for example, sitting in his seat and not acting negative, defiant or resistant. The entire class is then involved in the pay-off of the game if the student plays (behaves) appropriately. The teacher in one class started the game by announcing to the class:

Henry has some trouble with sitting still and this makes it hard for him to learn things. So, starting today, every afternoon we are going to play a good behavior game with Henry. And all of you can play and help Henry to be one of the best behaved children in the whole class.

The good behavior game works like this: When Henry sits in his own seat and pays attention, he will earn trinkets, candies and treats for the whole class. See this clock sitting on the desk in the front of the room? This is Henry's good behavior clock and it tells when Henry is being good. When Henry is sitting at his own desk or doing what he's supposed to do, the hands of the clock will move. When the hands are moving, it means that Henry is earning treats for the whole class. Each time the slow hand passes a number, Henry will earn one treat, and every treat that he earns will go into the "Sharing Jar." Fifteen minutes before the end of the day, Henry will pass out the treats that he has earned to the class. He will pass them out by rows, giving one to each person until he doesn't have any treats left. If the clock never stops, Henry will be able to earn at least one treat for each person in the class every day.

The clock will run whenever Henry is sitting at his desk or doing what he's supposed to do. (He should be at his own desk if the class is doing desk work.) But, if Henry misbehaves, I will have to turn off the clock. And when the hands of the clock are not moving, Henry isn't earning any treats for anyone. If you want him to earn a large number of treats, you can help by not paying attention to him when he makes noise, gets out of his chair without permission, or walks around the room.

One last thing. Not only can Henry earn treats for himself, and the rest of you. Henry will also receive a "red, good behavior star" each time the slow hand on the clock reaches the red star on top of the clock. And we will put all of his red stars on his "Good Behavior Progress Chart" in the front of the room.[2]

Initially Henry received a treat everyday. In order to improve his behavior, it was necessary to make him earn enough treats so that everyone had one before he received one.

Little is actually known about the effect of games upon student behavior. What is most striking is the fact that these games are apparently as popular with the children whose behavior is being changed as they are with teachers and administrators who desire the change. Students generally ask to play the game more, particularly when they have the opportunity to choose the peers on their team.[3]

It has been noted that:

> While game-like techniques are certainly not new to the classroom, an experimental analysis of their effects on behavior is unique. It may follow that an understanding of the mechanisms of the game, e.g., peer competition, group consequences vs. individual consequences, etc., together with research designed to enhance the significance of winning, by pairing winning with privileges, could lead to a set of effective and practical techniques of classroom behavior management based on games.[4]

Each of these games is devised for use with children whose behavior is not responsive to other teaching approaches and has previously led to exclusion from class. For some children it is necessary to combine a good behavior game with a time-out procedure.

Using a planned time out. Removing a child from the classroom or restricting him from an activity is another procedure for dealing with defiant outbursts and disruptive, aggressive behavior. This procedure not only relieves the teacher for brief periods of time from the pressure of such a youngster, but also aids the youngster whose behavior often leads to poor learning, exclusion from school, and negative reaction from parents and teachers.

The procedure, labeled "planned time out" or "antiseptic bouncing,"[5] has been used in schools for some time and there are a number of variations for its use. Basically, the procedure entails the removal of a child from a conflict situation where his behavior has exceeded the rules and expressed limits of acceptability.

One variation of the procedure allows for the disruptive child to be removed from the classroom to a place that does not connote punishment so that the child can regain his self-control. The child can be asked to leave the room for a few minutes to get a drink, wash up or deliver a message.[6] For example, the teacher can work out an arrangement with another member of the school staff—resource teacher, counselor, librarian, even the secretary or custodian—that the child will be sent to them for a few minutes, perhaps with a note to deliver, when he needs to settle down away from the classroom.

A second way to use this procedure assumes that the classroom provides activities that the child likes and wants to be a part of. Removing him from the classroom to a time-out room (e.g., a small room near the classroom) takes him away from these activities. This method is particularly useful when the child's defiance is increasing as a result of what is going on in the classroom (i.e., attention from teacher and/or peers).[7] The teacher should explain to the child that the purpose of removing him is to help him calm down and gain control of himself and that he can leave the time-out area and return to the classroom when he feels his behavior is under control.

Another variation of the time-out procedure involves telling children how to behave appropriately whenever they are misbehaving. If a child continues to behave inappropriately, he should be warned: "You are not supposed to be doing x. You are supposed to be doing y. If you do not change, you will be taken to the quiet room." Following the warning, the teacher should ignore the child for 15 seconds to allow him time to make the desired change. After that, if no definite move is made to end the unacceptable behavior and to begin the suggested activity, the child should be taken to the quiet room, where he is to remain for five minutes.[8]

A somewhat more concrete method of educating the disruptive child to the fact that his behavior will lead to "time out" from pleasurable class activities employs a red light mounted on the child's desk. The teacher first specifies the child's behavioral difficulties; for example, being out of his seat and unauthorized talking. The teacher then tells the child: "If you want to get out of your seat, or if you have something to say, please raise your hand and ask permission. Every time you are out of your seat, and every time you talk, this light will go on. Each time this light goes on, you must lose five minutes of gym time or recess, which must be spent in the (isolation) booth." This procedure can be used only for one 15-minute interval at some time during each day (if in the morning, time out could occur during recess; if after recess, time out could occur during lunch, etc.). Each time the child gets out of his seat or talks, the button is pushed to turn on the light for a second or so. Later in the day, during gym time or recess, the child is required to sit in a time-out booth for five minutes for each time the light has been turned on. The time-out booth could be outside of the classroom in the hallway and the child should not be allowed to take any materials into the booth. This procedure can be modified for use without the light. The teacher can merely write the child's name on the blackboard and place a mark beside it each time he misbehaves. The rest of the time-out procedure is still utilized.[9] This same method can be employed to increase attentive behaviors (see Chapter 2).

Some defiant outbursts must be stopped immediately. Two teachers working together can accomplish this and help the defiant child regain his self-control. When a child becomes unmanageable, he can be sent to a second teacher's room, given a seat in the back, and excluded from interaction or participation. After about one-half hour, he should be able to return to his classroom. At the kindergarten to second-grade level, a child who refuses to leave can be carried out by two teachers; older children can be informed that their parents will be phoned immediately.

> If the plan is to maximize the child's chances of remembering and following classroom rules, it must be introduced to the whole class not as an angry punitive retaliation by a distraught teacher, but as a way of helping children to remember to follow rules that allow them to enjoy learning. It should be explained that a child will be excluded not because he is unwanted or disliked, but because he needs a brief opportunity in another classroom to reflect on the rules he has been disobeying.[10]

Rather than remove a child from the classroom when the situation reaches the point where the teacher is furious, the teacher should give the child one warning which clearly states that if his behavior continues he will be removed from the classroom. A child should not be excluded without one private warning. If the child continues to defy the warning, the teacher should lead him out of the room and tell the entire class in his presence why he is being removed. After the teacher returns to the class, he should then review the situation with the rest of the class, emphasizing the reasons behind the rules and discussing alternative ways the child might have acted. The aim of this discussion is to enlist the support of the class in helping the excluded child. After school, the teacher can schedule a short meeting with the child so that he can explain that removal was to help the child remember class rules rather than to embarrass him. The teacher should let the child know that he hopes that in the future a warning will be enough to have the child control his own behavior, and emphasize that it is the child himself who decides whether he is excluded, not the teacher. Throughout the entire interaction with the child, it is necessary for the teacher to clearly express affection. This procedure is an effective technique for children through grade four.

> Especially when applied as calmly and consistently as possible in a program of relationship building the exclusion plan can greatly reduce mounting classroom tension in a relatively antiseptic way ...the procedure is to be explained in a period of relative calm by all the teachers on the same day if possible, singling no one out in its explanation or implementation. Every effort should be made by the teachers to present it as a way of giving students a chance to think over school rules rather than as a clever triumph by the school over troublemakers.[11]

The purpose of each of these alternative approaches is to establish external standards, teach appropriate behaviors and clarify consequences for children who act as if they do not have, or do not think to use, internal standards for coping with frustration or negative feelings. Clarifying rules and teaching appropriate behaviors by playing good behavior games and using time out are procedures designed to head off more negative consequences (e.g., exclusion from school), which often occur because such children lose control or seem unable to contain themselves without these planned intervention techniques.

Providing structure and predictability

Often the student who is most prone to be defiant is least able to take part in, and profit from, verbal discussion. As one teacher indicated: "I don't think discussion works with the *extremely* defiant student. I don't think they're able to, in their own minds, think things out. These students often don't seem to be able to apply what has been discussed to their own behavior. This is the kind of child you do not just teach the rules; you have to show them. They have to experience the results of their behavior before they know where the puzzle pieces fit. You have to take them by the hand and show them everything. They have to touch and feel and see the consequences of their defiance to be able to learn new ways. At times their verbal negativism is due to the fact that they are just sitting in the class, lost to what is going on around them. To intervene with these children, instructions and ideas should be presented slowly, with an emphasis upon clarity, written on the board, discussed and reexplained." The issue of instructions has also been discussed in other chapters, and those techniques are appropriate here.

There have been efforts to provide a specific "total" classroom environment for the most troubled of these youngsters. These environments have been called a "total therapeutic setting,"[12] an "ordered environment" with a "structured approach."[13,14] Teaching techniques which contribute to a total classroom environment are presented below.

For children who are unable to control their own impulses, who are physically and verbally aggressive and who are unable to foresee consequences, assignments should be brief and fully defined, with verbal explanation specific and minimal, and enough time given for the child to complete every task. Materials should be limited and laid out before-hand with directions demonstrated in a step-by-step fashion. These children often find "very rigid, unimaginative, highly structured methods more acceptable and less frightening than open-ended creative fantasy-arousing types of tasks, such as play acting or storytelling."[15]

Teaching techniques and materials which provide "clear direction, firm expectations and consistent follow-through" are helpful in dealing with children who display hyperactive, distractible, attention-getting and uncooperative behavior. A child who often teases others and roams about when he is not occupied should be given a specific activity to do rather than allowed to be idle and to fall back on his own judgment. If a child blows up emotionally (but does not cause harm to him-self or others), the teacher should not become involved with him, but instead give him time to calm down by himself. Once calmed, he can then return to his work. If he cannot calm down, time out from the group may be necessary until he is able to maintain control. Because these children are often easily distracted (see Chapter 2, Increasing Attentive-ness), all unnecessary activity and out-of-seat behavior should be halted. Material should be presented in as definite, specific and concrete a way as possible, assignments broken into a series of short tasks and, whenever possible, the child shown rather than told what to do. When he *completely* finishes each task, the teacher can check his work and give him the next task. Assignments should be completed exactly according to instructions; if poorly completed, they should be redone.

The child should be given ample time to get work started. If he does not start the work after one reminder by the teacher, he should be told that he must complete the work before he can do anything else (e.g., play, move around). As long as the teacher feels that an assignment is reasonable, he should consistently hold to its completion even in the face of the child's refusal. The teacher should not accept a child's decision not to do work, or "I'll do it later," but should follow through to make certain that he does an assignment exactly as he is asked.[16]

The complete routine of a structured classroom works to prevent the recurrence of disruptive behaviors. Almost nothing is left to chance. As in the examples above, the focus of the teaching techniques is upon providing a totally predictable environment to abet behavior control.

In contrast to this approach are the approaches outlined earlier in this chapter—spelling out rules, airing dissent, providing alternatives—which stress the importance of allowing some leeway and room for choice for the youngster displaying negative feelings. These different points of view are probably due to the severity of disturbance and type of child. Proponents of the structured approach have focused attention upon the seriously disturbed or brain-damaged child. Nevertheless, the teacher and consulting psychologist should be familiar with both modes of approach since either one or both may be helpful and necessary to designing a plan for a particular child. All of the research concerning teaching these youngsters is in agreement that predictability and clarity of instructions are crucial if the youngsters are to succeed academically as well as behaviorally.

Dealing with accompanying emotions

Because of the nature of defiant behaviors, it is imperative that the teacher realistically face his own feelings when working with defiant youngsters. As noted earlier, these behaviors can lead to a disruption in the relationship between child and teacher, with negative feelings on both sides. Negative statements are in and of themselves usually viewed as an attack, whether they are directly focused (e.g., "You are stupid") or indirectly focused (e.g., "English is stupid"; "That was a dumb thing to say").

One way to help the defiant child gain an understanding of the negative feelings he creates is to role-play specific problem situations in a small group of children. The teacher can play the part of an abusive, negative and defiant child, while the children take turns playing the role of the teacher.

For example, the teacher as pupil can say: "You won't get me to do the work. No matter what you do, I'm not going to do it." The children must then devise methods to deal with what is, in reality, their *own* behavior. In the course of such activities, the teacher can ask how they reacted to the teacher's being defiant, and explain that such an attitude can hurt the teacher's feelings or the feelings of others.

Perhaps even more important is the need for the teacher to be realistic about his own feelings and attempt to understand how the defiant child is manipulating the situation. The teacher should be willing to raise questions about how a response he makes to the child reflects his own feelings of hurt and anger. He can review the strategies presented here which might enable a different relationship to develop, and attempt to create a set of responses which do not put the child in a position where he feels he must defy the teacher. If, for example, the teacher finds himself, upon turning around to a noisy classroom, consistently "catching" his most defiant pupil in misbehavior, he might consider re-examining his vision. Even if, in the particular case, his vision were 20-20 (the child was defiant), he should ask himself if on other occasions he has been myopic because he lost sight of his plan and the many alternatives available when confronted by such behavior. Children whose behavior is characterized by defiance cause loss of perspective in even the best of teachers. Arbitrary punishment or punishment in front of the group leads only to increased defiance. The teacher must remember that the child's behavior is telling him that the student is just as unhappy with the teacher and the school as the teacher may be with the defiant child. The teacher has planned with him, discussed with him, listened to him, but they have not found the solution, and therefore both feel the failure.

Using outside resources

In most school settings outside help is limited. In an effort to help the especially defiant and negative child, an established relationship with the parent is particularly important. A visit to the child's home to speak with his parents as early in the school year as possible may help. It is best to call to make an appointment to visit them at home, rather than ask them to come to school. The teacher should not discuss the child's bad behavior with the parents as the initial focus of their meeting. Because of this he will probably be the first teacher who does not dwell upon the negative. He should get to know the parents and let them know him. He can establish himself as a person they can talk to and work with. He may well find that the parents are also having difficulty coping with the child's defiance. They will be more willing to work with the teacher if they see him as an ally and as one who is sincere in his desire to teach their child. This interaction will also give clues as to the cause of some of the child's negative feelings. Whether the teacher discovers the parents to be a potential source of help or a major cause of the child's problem, meeting with the parents will provide insight. As one teacher who tried this approach indicated, "You can be much more understanding of the child if you know why he is feeling so negative."

A second, often untapped source of help is a fellow teacher. Since certain standards must be developed and maintained with regard to defiant and aggressively negative behavior if learning is to occur, exclusion from the classroom may become necessary in extreme situations. The teacher should arrange a reciprocal agreement with another teacher to accept the defiant child into the second classroom, without attention or fanfare. This approach has been discussed earlier in this chapter as a time-out procedure.

Summary

While children in special classes are more apt to show negative feelings, the teacher must be alert to the fact that planning for these children is often necessary in any regular class. These youngsters can be the most difficult to cope with, and offer the greatest challenge to teacher and school. In particular they challenge the teacher as an authority. Defiant behaviors occur in all normal school settings; however, their relation to academic failure is clearest in teacher-subject-matter centered classroom settings in which teacher authority and decision-making are predominant, and in which little decision-making is shared with the student or choice allowed him. In classes where student activity is not only allowed but supported and encouraged, where student interest and individual differences are highlighted, where the student spends an appreciable amount of time in learning activities with peers (not involving specific leadership and direct interaction with the teacher) such behaviors do not constitute a breach in learning efficiency. However, the more troubled child may need structure, predictability and teacher control, at least initially.

When teaching such children there are two issues to consider: (1) the use of teaching strategies that decrease the child's need to be negative and defiant; and (2) planning an environment in which academic success and teacher-pupil relationships are possible in spite of such behaviors. For these purposes there are a wide variety of alternatives available for the needs of each youngster. Before the teacher falls back on the old saw, "I've tried everything and nothing works with this student," it is recommended that this and other chapters be reread. Following rereading (and discussion with other teachers), a new plan of approach should be created. Many techniques which work for most children need modification or important additions for other children. This should be kept in mind whenever a teaching plan is created, especially when working with the more aggressively negative children.

The approaches which might be used with these children include careful clarification of classroom rules *before* they are broken, rather than after. As much as possible the child should be involved in establishing rules. Consequences should be defined and consistently carried out when rules are broken. It must be established that the teacher will also abide by commitments to the students. When the focus is academic work, instructions for these youngsters should be simple and many examples provided. Their frustration level is often very low and their view of the teacher and work tasks negative. It is necessary to assure them that every effort will be made to keep them out of positions where they will be lost, embarrassed, and unsupported.

There are games which can be adapted for any classroom to teach appropriate behaviors. It must not be assumed that simply because there are rules, every child knows how to behave and to live within those rules. Many children have a narrow range of behavioral responses to real-life problem situations. If a negative, defiant child can learn alternative responses, he will be less likely to react with others in negative or angry ways.

At times, it is necessary to remove some of these children from the classroom. A carefully planned time-out procedure is one of the alternative methods which can be utilized as a preventive measure. Removal from the classroom need not be used, as it often is, as a last resort, leading to rather dire consequences (e.g., expulsion from school, etc.). In fact, planned removal to a time-out room or other classroom can increase productive behavior and decrease both time lost from learning and alienation of feelings between student and teacher. Another way to diminish the potency of defiant behavior is to divert the youngster with an alternative activity within the classroom so that no confrontation occurs. Diversions are best when they are designed to enable the child to do what he wanted to do but in an acceptable manner or place.

When the expression of negative feelings is accepted in the classroom, there is less interference with learning than in settings where dissent is not allowed. This is important because academic performance is enhanced by the decrease in negative feelings and behaviors of these youngsters. The teacher must also recognize that more than any other set of behaviors, negative feelings and actions bring about unhappy emotional responses from the teacher himself. An angry emotional response from the teacher reduces the possibility that the many alternative approaches can be called into play.

In view of the fact that children with such behaviors can be expected in almost all classes, and that these children are more apt than any other group to upset the teacher, knowledge of the range of potential alternative responses is essential to the children's academic success and to the teacher's effectiveness.

Footnotes

[1] J. W. Giebink, D. O. Stover and M. A. Fahl. Teaching adaptive responses to frustration to emotionally disturbed boys. *Journal of Consulting and Clinical Psychology*, 1968, *32*, 366-368.

[2] E. S. Kubany, L. E. Weiss and B. B. Sloggett. The good behavior clock: A reinforcement time out procedure for reducing disruptive behavior. *Journal of Behavior Therapy and Experimental Psychiatry*, 1971, *2*, 173-179.

[3] W. J. Gnagey, P. L. Goodwin, E. H. Jabker, K. B. Shaw and M. P. McCormick. The use of group and individual rewards to reduce deviance in a high school classroom. Unpublished manuscript, 1971.

[4] H. H. Barrish, M. Saunders and M. M. Wolf. Good behavior game: Effects of individual contingencies for group consequences on disruptive behavior in a classroom. *Journal of Applied Behavior Analysis*, 1969, *2*, 119-124.

[5] F. Redl and D. Wineman. *Controls from within*. Glencoe: The Free Press, 1952, pp. 198-209.

[6] N. J. Long and R. G. Newman. A differential approach to the management of surface behavior of children in school. *Bulletin of the School of Education of Indiana University*, 1961, *37*, 47-61.

[7] R. F. Whelan and N. G. Haring. Modification in maintenance of

behavior through systematic application of consequences. Paper presented at 43rd Annual Convention of the Council for Exceptional Children, 1965.

8 B. H. Wasik, K. Senn, R. H. Welch and B. R. Cooper. Behavior modification with culturally deprived school children: Two case studies. *Journal of Applied Behavior Analysis*, 1969, *2*, 181-194.

9 E. Ramp, R. Ulrich and S. Dulaney. Delayed time out as a procedure for reducing disruptive classroom behavior: A case study. *Journal of Applied Behavior Analysis*, 1971, *4*, 235-239.

10 S. B. Sarason, M. Levine, I. I. Goldenberg, D. L. Cherlin and E. M. Bennett. *Psychology in community settings*. New York: John Wiley and Sons, 1966, p. 142.

11 Ibid., pp. 144-145.

12 R. G. Newman. The assessment of progress in the treatment of hyperaggressive children with learning disturbances within a school setting. *American Journal of Orthopsychiatry*, 1959, *29*, 633-643.

13 N. Haring and E. Phillips. *Educating emotionally disturbed children*. New York: McGraw-Hill, 1962, pp. 60-65.

14 P. A. Gallagher. Structuring academic tasks for emotionally disturbed boys. *Exceptional Children*, 1972, *38*, 711-720.

15 R. G. Newman. The acting out boy. *Exceptional Children*, 1956, *22*, 186-190, 204-216.

16 Haring and Phillips, pp. 153-154.

9 Allaying Achievement Anxiety

The behaviors of concern here indicate that the youngster is becoming anxious or emotionally upset at times when he is asked to demonstrate what he knows, to give information or merely to express a point of view. His voice may quiver, he may look toward the ground, and may speak in such a low voice that it is difficult to hear him. The youngster is obviously ill at ease in such situations, and he may block his thinking and forget what he was going to say, making matters even worse.

Signs of anxiety may also emerge when the teacher attempts to correct or assist the student in his work. The child is quick to see such attempts to help him as criticisms of his work, and he reacts as though accused of having failed or being "stupid." He may get angry or sulk, or sigh and act defeated. This hypersensitivity to any implications of failure may occur whenever he is having difficulty understanding or producing something. He cannot persist in a reasonably calm mood, but gets flooded with anxiety which interferes with his problem-solving skills. Correction of his work is viewed not as assistance in his education, but as a direct and personal attack upon him.

If a test is given, he manifests and usually verbally

admits to anxiety and worry about how well he will do. The mere announcement that a test will be given in the future may elicit all sorts of worries and expletives. If he does not do as well as he wished to do on a test, there are overt signs of concern and trepidation. Younger children may more openly exhibit anxiety through tears, older youngsters through anxious looks or flushed facial expressions. In all of this there is a fear of failure, and a tense expectation that their work will be judged inadequate.

The behaviors reflecting this dimension are not limited to test situations or only to classrooms where tests are given. The overt display of anxiety occurs in all school settings, including open classrooms and special education classes. In these settings and in kindergarten and first grade where tests as such are not given, these behaviors occur when the student must in some way perform, meet a standard or display what he knows. This can be seen by the teacher in a number of situations. When a new activity or task is introduced he may hold back, need added support to get him started, or indicate verbally or by his actions that he feels he cannot cope with the expectations made of him. During a "show-and-tell" period or other group activities he may be reluctant to take part or may wish to do something else rather than involve himself in a situation where his work might be judged.

In all these behaviors there is emotional arousal and tension that *interferes with the learning process.* When this child is challenged to pit himself against some standard of academic excellence, his anxiety does not bring about a mobilization of resources to help him perform. The youngster is not alerted to the problem, and he does not draw effectively upon his memory. His mind goes blank and thoughts may race uncontrollably through his head. His thinking may quickly center not on the questions and answers at issue, but rather on his expected failure, his inability to think straight, or how foolish and embarrassed he feels and must appear to others.

Youngsters who characteristically respond this way have

a keen awareness of expected "external" standards of academic achievement. Thus, they often dread school as a place where much is expected of them and where they too often do not measure up. They suffer from low self-esteem and develop self-derogatory attitudes, depending upon the degree to which self-esteem has become associated with academic success in their lives. Confronted with a demand for competent performance in class, their low self-esteem leads them to expect failure and to become anxious. This anxiety reflects a degree of self-concern that becomes an obstacle to subsequent thinking. Rather than mustering all his resources to solve the academic problem, the youngster gets caught up in thinking about his own incompetence, how "stupid" he feels and everyone must think he is. Overconcern about the self often moves to the physical level, and these children are more prone than their peers to make frequent visits to the school nurse or to complain of not feeling well.

Having focused upon the behaviors that define this negative anxiety dimension and its underlying processes, it is important to differentiate it from other behaviors that may appear similar but in fact have a different meaning. At times, youngsters manifest anxiety and apparent overconcern about their schoolwork which have positive rather than negative implications for achievement. Some youngsters are concerned that they master all the details of something before they are satisfied that they are right. If the teacher gives an assignment, they will want to double-check or to have the directions repeated or clarified to make sure they completely understand them (they usually do). When the youngster turns in his work, the teacher may find the assignment carried out well beyond the minimum requirement. This overconcern with meeting expectations suggests the same hypersensitivity to standards and concern with success and failure characteristic of the achievement anxiety dimension. The difference is that the behaviors just noted reflect anxiety turned into positive academic performance. They do not lead to self-concern and inability to focus on academic problems, but rather intensify problem-solving and enhance achievement.

There is another frequently occurring type of behavior that may easily be misconstrued as reflecting achievement anxiety, but in fact does not. This behavior may be manifested in numerous ways, but all suggest the youngster's concern with getting good grades. As report cards or parent conferences approach, the youngster questions the teacher about his probable mark in the course. He may make it clear that he wishes and "needs" a better grade, or even react strongly when a grade (or test score) is lower than he expected. In general, such concern about grades is not to be confused with achievement anxiety. The concern with the outward signs of achievement is a realistic one for most youngsters who must confront both peers and parents at report–card time. Grades still reflect an academic social situation which is basically competitive, and in such a system grades are a major weapon for the youngster in the competitive battle. The concern is realistic and, in fact, more likely to occur among those who are achieving fairly well. This should not be surprising, for the youngster who is sure he will not receive a good grade will more likely want to forget the whole thing, and will probably not be the one to raise questions about his grades.

Finally, achievement anxiety, as presently discussed, is not an implied state. We are all prone to infer the presence of a variety of emotions and moods in children, particularly children who are less verbal or more withdrawn than their classmates. Achievement anxiety as discussed here is manifest openly both in words and nonverbal ways, identifiable by any observant teacher, and it is this overt and conscious form which can cause lowered achievement.

In spite of the relationship between high levels of anxiety and school failure experiences, little substantiated information exists about specific teaching strategies to allay achievement anxiety. Many teachers are limited in their awareness of the nature and meaning of student behaviors reflecting anxiety, and are also unaware of the aspects of their classroom program which stimulate or increase such anxiety. Yet, there is evidence that a child's anxiety about achievement is highly related to the teacher's approach to that child and his classmates. After examining teacher-student interactions, the question has been posed:

> Would this child experience anxiety if his performance was not being evaluated by the teacher or examiner—by an adult whom the child perceives as a person of authority from whom a negative evaluation would arouse more than feelings of disappointment?. . . We assumed that without the presence of the teacher the child would not experience anxiety (which is often the case when the regular teacher is absent and there is a substitute for the day). The teacher is, of course, an important person for all children in her classroom, but for the test anxious child she possessed an unusual degree of importance and power which, so to speak, is granted her by the child.[1]

Alternative Teaching Strategies

When confronted with a child who is overly anxious about his work and at times seems to underestimate his ability, it is natural to want to comfort and support him. The teacher attempts to say things that will make him feel better: "Don't worry. You'll do all right" or "We all get nervous sometimes. You're not alone. Other students feel the same way." The teacher might also consider saying: "I make mistakes too" or "No one is perfect."

While such attempts may do no harm, it is doubtful whether they do any good either. The child who is anxious usually receives little solace from knowing that others also might be uncomfortable. Anxiety inhibits perspective, and the child remains wrapped up in his own discomfort. Such attempts at reassurance may also backfire: the youngster may feel that the teacher does not want to consider how he feels. To him the teacher *seems* to be saying that his anxiety is not important and should be turned off, and that his inability to be calm makes him personally less acceptable. The child also gets these feelings when he is pressed to talk about his worries or is questioned about them in front of the group.

Nor does it help when he is told that "Everything will be all right if you try to do better next time" or that "If you study harder you'll get it."

The teaching strategies presented in this chapter often reflect the understanding that anxiety can be decreased when pressure to produce for an authority is decreased. Achievement is also fostered for many anxious children when they are afforded the opportunity to talk with an understanding adult about their fears, apprehensions and opinions.

Private talks
between teacher and student

With many children, anxiety can be reduced by the teacher's reassuring smile, touch, or arm around the shoulder. By sitting next to an anxious child, the teacher can help reduce tension and communicate a willingness to protect as well as teach. Such youngsters can feel supported in knowing that the teacher realizes how they feel, is willing to be close to them, but maintains confidence in them: "Everything new we try in the classroom you won't get every time. Sometimes you'll worry about that and sometimes you won't. Just keep working along with me and I'll help you get it. No one is going to laugh at anyone else or criticize."

Very early in working with the anxious student it is useful to talk with him specifically about his fear of failure and his anxiety when he has to perform. If done with understanding and willingness to listen to and accept the child's opinions, such talk can help to decrease the occurrence of other difficulties associated with fear, such as withdrawal, aggressive behavior, or loss of desire to have a relationship with the teacher.

Private talks can also help in other ways. The teacher may explore with the youngster what particular circumstances in the classroom precipitate his anxiety (e.g., whenever he thinks people won't understand him or he'll say something wrong) as well as the youngster's view of his anxiety and its relationship to schoolwork. Does he think that the teacher will scold him or not like him? What does he like about school and the classroom? What doesn't he like about school? Does he cry sometimes in school? What makes him feel like crying? What does he worry about sometimes? It is often useful to explore what in particular touched off his anxiety that afternoon; what in particular about the test upset him; when the nervousness began, and so forth. The teacher may discover that the youngster's anxious feelings are associated with parental standards or sibling rivalry (external standards at home), fear of being laughed at in the classroom, or specific academic content areas in which standards are unusually high or skills low. It is also useful to explore those settings in which the youngster feels relaxed or secure and those topics about which he can talk comfortably. Analyzing all of this, as well as contrasting settings that do or do not arouse anxiety, offers the teacher direction in choosing helpful teaching strategies.

The causes and effects surrounding a youngster's achievement anxiety should be discussed with him, affording him insights into his own behavior, these in turn affording him some feeling of control over his worries. When the youngster learns to recognize his anxious feelings and knows how to avoid or minimize them, these feelings are then predictable or even manipulable. The youngster may have suggestions as to how his anxiety level may be reduced, or useful opinions about what the teacher suggests. It is comforting to the youngster to know that the teacher understands his feelings and is willing to work with him to do something about them. This is probably in marked contrast to other concerned adults who have attempted to help by saying that these feelings are "silly," or in some other way suggesting that they are unreasonable or unacceptable.

Providing a reasonably
pressure-free environment

Teachers should be aware that a child's anxious feelings indicate that he feels unable to perform perfectly. Consequently, without planned intervention, his efforts are impeded by fear of making mistakes or of complete failure. These youngsters often feel that they can never please the adult in the learning setting. They become upset when an adult attempts to correct or question their thoughts or work. Therefore, the teacher should create an atmosphere in which the pressure to be perfect is greatly reduced. Competition to be "first" or "right" should be replaced with leadership indicating "Let's see if we can find out together."

The youngster should initially be protected from the usual symbols of competitive pressure, such as comparison with more successful peers. Pressure is also decreased when the teacher marks papers by highlighting what is correct more than what is incorrect. Grades can be replaced by comments at the top of the page. Allowance should be made for the student to make comments as well. Highly anxious students often achieve better when they are encouraged to make comments about a test or test items. This opportunity to comment also serves to release tension and to help the student to feel that he has an accepting, unpressuring teacher who is more interested in him and his thinking than in his test score. The student's achievement may be aided when he views his teacher "as a friendly person who wishes to encourage communication, rather than as a powerful authority figure who arbitrarily and punitively assigns grades."[2] The use of teaching approaches that decrease pressure puts the importance of tests in its proper perspective, and red marking pencils can be dispensed with. Correction and evaluation of student work may be made in the context of communication between teacher and student rather than as a teacher passing judgment upon a student.

Class participation can be conducted so that the competitive raising of hands is avoided. The anxious youngster can be helped by letting him know a little beforehand that he will be called on, and for what reason. The teacher can prepare him by referring him to a place where he can refresh his memory while other students are working on something else. "Remember when we talked about Columbus? He had three ships. Look for the part of the story that tells about his ships. When you find it, you can tell the others where to look. They will be ready to find out tomorrow."

When a youngster feels that he must know the correct answer, know it fast, and then worry whether his knowledge or lack of it will cause him embarrassment, his anxiety level is substantially increased. In instances of severe anxiety about reciting, the teacher may "contract" with the youngster not to call upon him without forewarning. The child then knows he will be prepared beforehand (e.g., "Can you help us solve this problem?") and at least initially will only be asked to respond in areas where the teacher feels that the youngster is able to contribute to the class discussion.

Anxious youngsters often know the material covered in class. Many are bright and capable. When this is the case, the teacher may point it out to the youngster when he has to perform: "You've shown me all week that you know this material and you'll do fine on this work, too" or "Just review what we did yesterday and everything will work out."

A good sense of humor is a great asset in working with the anxious youngster. Telling a good joke or being able to laugh is always a source of tension release, and helps a youngster forget himself for the moment. Laughter eases pressure and conveys to a youngster that he can relax a bit.

Since the need to demonstrate knowledge is always part of any classroom and mistakes are inevitable, we must all learn to live with making mistakes. However, the anxious youngster does not live with the belief that "I will make errors sometimes," but with the fear that something will always go wrong. His anxiety is so much a part of him that not only is his academic success decreased, but also his self-esteem as a pleasing and potentially productive person is diminished.

Fostering self-esteem

Teaching techniques that foster a sense of accomplishment and self-confidence are useful to employ with any child. They are, however, particularly necessary with the anxious child since his anxiety relates intimately to his expectation of failure. Any experiences in the classroom, therefore, that afford him a feeling of success are crucial.

> Some educational psychologists see one of the primary roles of the skillful teacher, especially in the elementary and secondary school years, as being to promote and sustain a positive self-concept in the child. This notion, as expressed in the work of developmental psychologists such as Havighurst and Erikson, is epigenetic in character. Expressed in another way, failure of the child to achieve the tasks characteristic of a particular developmental stage through which he is passing is thought to be inimical to his progress towards adulthood. If high anxiety interferes with academic achievement (an important developmental task), and if teachers are unable to identify the high-anxious child and take steps to promote a more positive self-concept, then it seems unlikely that the anxious child will achieve a positive sense of identity, a goal which many psychologists see as being necessary for successful personality development in childhood and adolescence.[3]

Whenever possible, it is important that the teacher point out the youngster's successes: "What you've done here is interesting. I like the words you used, and how you did it." Initially it is best not to point up what is incorrect. It is also important never to praise when it is unwarranted. When a child has actually failed, he needs encouragement, not empty praise; unwarranted praise only makes the youngster feel worse, conveying that the teacher thinks he needs praise no matter what he can or cannot do. Praise must bear a direct relationship to something he really can do or did do.

> It is crucial that the teacher recognize the difference between praise and encouragement. Praise is usually given to a child when a task or deed is well done, or when the task is completed. Encouragement is needed when the child fails. Encouraging the child during the task or for trying is as important as giving the child recognition at the completion of the task. If the child is once rewarded with praise, then the withholding or lack of praise signifies failure. Flattery may promote insecurity as the child may

become frightened of the possibility of not being able to live up to expectations or not sure of always getting the same kind of praise again. The child has the mistaken idea that *unless he is praised, he has no value,* and therefore he is a failure. Praise puts the emphasis on the child, encouragement emphasizes the task.[4]

Any youngster can experience success and the reward that success provides if the teacher takes care in structuring tasks so that the youngster will be able to proceed with some expectation of success. Often it is possible to afford opportunities for him to perform in areas where he has knowledge or particular skill. If a youngster has talent, this too can be used as a vehicle through which he can gain prestige and deserving flattery. When a teacher can recognize the behaviors that indicate anxiety, he can direct the anxious student to other classroom activities in which the student feels more secure.

Encouraging performance
with tolerable anxiety

Reality dictates that these children must learn to tolerate some anxiety. Apprehension is inevitable in the educational process. Once the teacher has created a reasonably pressure-free environment, it is then necessary to develop techniques to foster the child's ability to tolerate anxiety and still perform academically.

It is easier to assist the anxious youngster to perform well with low tension when the situation is structured to avoid the concept of "right" and "wrong." The stage can be set by raising questions to which the teacher acknowledges that even he does not know the answer. The child can be asked how he thinks "we might find out what we want to know" with the intent to demonstrate that knowing the right answer is not as important as being willing to ask and seek to find out. The teacher conveys to the child by word and action that school is a place where questions and exploration are freely encouraged. The teacher must provide for the child a model of someone who tolerates "not knowing" by being curious and open in his own approach to problems and quest for answers. A classroom discussion might focus on how ideas differ or how people react differently in the same situation. A question might be posed to the class which requires as many and varied answers as possible.

It is also possible to handle evaluation of performance and tests so as to reduce their anxiety-provoking elements. Fact tests may be used less often. In many subjects, experimentation may by used for evaluation rather than tests. If fact tests are to be used, it is helpful to have the youngster make up some of the questions or to have the class make up the entire test. Tests can be presented as games with no time limits or reading required.[5] The anxious child is also more apt to be successful when test items are arranged in an order of increasing difficulty proceeding from what the child already knows to what the teacher wants to know about his learning.[6] Anxiety is decreased and achievement increased when the children are told that the purpose of the test is to find out whether the teaching has been good, or whether the questions are too hard or too easy. In this context, the youngsters can also evaluate their own performance, lessening the obvious input of adult standards. However, when they are told that the purpose of the test is to report to parents or others about how well they are doing, their anxiety is increased and their learning is decreased.

Since anxiety derives in large part from anticipation of inability to cope with classroom demands, all techniques are useful which enhance the youngster's feeling that he can control and/or predict these demands. If the anxious youngster must perform, he may be asked to perform only for a small group of peers he knows well. Making up his own tests is also useful from this perspective. It is also helpful to allow the youngster some choice about when he will be evaluated. The teacher may wish to establish a signaling system so that the youngster can tell him when he feels comfortable enough to recite or make a presentation. At least initially, the teacher might agree with the youngster that he will not be called upon in class unless he raises his hand or in some other way indicates he wants to say something. Each of these approaches is predicated upon the realization that the child must learn to perform in the classroom and that to do so he must be assisted to tolerate the anxiety that participation brings.

A child can be taught to increase his ability to tolerate anxiety created by a classroom situation or a teacher's behavior. For example, if a teacher feels that it is necessary to raise his voice to handle some classroom situations, the anxious child may respond by not trying to complete a problem because he fears that his mistakes might cause the teacher to yell at him. An effort should be made to help him to feel more in control and less threatened by the teacher. The child can be told that the teacher will yell at him when he makes a mistake. Then the teacher can ask him to deliberately make an error. When the teacher yells at the child, the yell should be in a loud, "mock" voice. The teacher can then ask the child, "Do I yell that loud?" After a discussion of the teacher's yelling, the process can be repeated by telling the child, "I'll try to yell even louder." This error-yelling is made into a game by asking the child to yell when the teacher makes an error. The effort is to allow the child to see that the teacher accepts his yelling, and that the teacher's yelling is tolerable and need not overwhelm him.[7]

There are other skills the youngster can be taught which will enhance the feeling that he can cope, especially when confronted with tests. For instance, he may be advised that he should read through all the questions on a test before answering any, then first answer those he knows the answers to, and so on through those he is unsure of. He can be instructed not to go back over questions he has already answered in order to decrease the possibility that he will become uncertain about even those which he initially thought were correct. These youngsters do not improve test performance by going back over their answers.

A number of reports have noted that anxious students perform successfully using individualized, self-instructional and programmed learning materials. Anxious children are

. . . more likely to make initiating responses in situations where they choose the task or the problem themselves and where they perform privately rather than in public. It might be argued that such children are more likely to show initiative, at least in early school, in auto-instructional rather than classroom settings. For children whose primary inhibitions appear to involve language, non-verbal tasks are more likely to elicit initiating behavior.[8]

Unlike the usual group activities in the classroom, self-instructional materials can be used to alleviate the pressure of doing things quickly to keep up with others. Errors can be made and corrected by the student himself without fear of negative evaluation of his work by others. This fosters exploration and decreases the need for public display of "right answers." Programmed materials present information in logical, carefully organized, small steps. Earlier steps are simpler than later steps, and when the youngster feels pressure mount he can return to earlier steps to review familiar ground. These materials provide immediate feedback to the student about how well he is doing. Such feedback has been found to facilitate learning for highly anxious children who typically find it difficult to accept criticism or correction from the teacher.

Summary

Heightened anxiety is related to lowered academic achievement and often signifies a diminished self-concept and negative or fearful feelings about the teacher, the school and peers. The teacher must intervene with teaching strategies which allay anxiety if learning is to occur.

In order to teach these youngsters it is important to be aware that behavioral signs of anxiety in the classroom are often overlooked and not understood. The first step toward fostering academic achievement is the clear recognition of signs of achievement-impeding anxiety. Few children can or will tell the teacher that they are afraid. Most show fear through maladaptive responses to classroom demands. Once the teacher identifies some of the behaviors described in this chapter (e.g., the child views attempts to correct work as criticism, he holds back from involvement in group activities, etc.), a productive first step is a personal talk with the youngster to indicate awareness of his tendency to worry about things. From this point on the aim is to communicate the ability to help by listening to the child and working with him in ways which do not stir up further anxiety. This should ultimately enable the student to form a positive picture of his relationship with the teacher and to feel that the teacher is someone he can please.

These youngsters perform best in low-pressure classrooms, free of concern with errors. Initially these youngsters need to feel protected: they are vulnerable to signs which indicate that they are less than perfect. Fear of making errors is diminished when they can discuss corrections as work to be redone to find out more about a subject, rather than as indicators of the inadequacy of their efforts. The feeling that someone understands or cares can grow when the teaching approach is changed from "You find the answer" to, "Let's find out together."

The public display of knowledge in a classroom group is stressful for these students. They fail to perform adequately because of emotional concerns, not lack of knowledge. However, their feeling is that they are less able than others and public embarrassment only serves to increase this sense of inadequacy. The anxious child is greatly in need of peer support but because of his difficulties is deprived of it, as well as other successes in school. When the child is enabled to see himself as capable and interesting to others, his self-esteem is greatly enhanced.

These students are apt to feel less anxious when the teacher's response is one which encourages their efforts in an ongoing manner rather than after full completion of work. It is important to focus encouragement upon what the youngster is doing rather than his quality as a person, and to use direct praise judiciously. Praise followed by periods of no

155

praise often leaves the anxious child with the feeling that he has done something wrong, or causes him to feel overwhelmed when correction of his work is necessary.

The teacher can offer the child the opportunity to control some of what happens to him. The child can be allowed to create items for his own tests, and to defer a presentation to a time when he feels ready. Learning can be enhanced for the anxious youngster by providing materials which enable him to work alone, to pace himself, and to check his errors. He learns to tolerate the fact that he will make errors, and also learns that his errors can be corrected. The purpose of evaluation and the review of work samples is to assess the child's learning, not his ability to tolerate anxiety.

Most important is the use of approaches which teach the youngster to tolerate some anxiety. It is most helpful if the teacher can provide a model of one who can tolerate tension, correction and not knowing all the answers. The teacher must indicate that he accepts the fact that some children need to do work in ways that are different. Thus, although work and learning expectations should be maintained for the anxious student, the form must often be changed. The anxious child should know that he is expected to demonstrate what he has learned, but that he may choose optional ways to perform.

Footnotes

[1] S. B. Sarason, K. S. Davidson, F. F. Lighthall, R. Waite and B. Ruebush. *Anxiety in elementary school children.* New York: John Wiley and Sons, 1960, p. 11.

[2] E. Gaudry and C. D. Spielberger. *Anxiety and educational achievement.* New York: John Wiley and Sons, 1971, p. 26.

[3] Ibid. p. 22.

[4] R. Dreikurs, D. B. Grunwald and F. C. Pepper. *Maintaining sanity in the classroom.* New York: Harper and Row, 1971, pp. 71-72.

[5] Sarason, et al., pp. 133-136.

[6] Gaudry and Spielberger, pp. 26-27.

[7] J. S. Bruner. *Toward a theory of instruction.* Cambridge, Massachusetts: Harvard University Press, 1966, p. 145.

[8] P. Mussen and C. D. Kuhlman. Initiating responses. In J. Bruner (Ed.), *Learning about learning.* USDHEW Cooperative Research Monograph No. 15, 1966, 14-27.

10 Meeting the Needs of the Restless, Socially Overinvolved Student

The behaviors contributing to this dimension are well known to all teachers: they involve restless and socially disruptive activity. Children who behave in this way seem unable to stay quiet for very long; they get out of their seats and move about the room when everyone else is seated. As if unable to accept being ignored, they cannot satisfy their restless urges alone or quietly. They make unnecessary noises by dropping pencils or books, or banging things. When seated they must tilt back their chairs, curl and uncurl their knees under them, or twist and turn. As a consequence, when quiet work is necessary, they annoy other children. Their noisemaking interrupts the concentration of those who want to work, and thus interrupts the work efficiency of the class.

The restless youngster generally needs to involve or be involved with peers. He interacts with classmates in ways that cannot be ignored, such as poking, teasing, or bumping into others as they walk by. While most youngsters are occasionally restless and might distract peers from their work, the more disturbing and restless student seems to have an added need to interact with and physically touch them. If someone else is moving about or making noise, this youngster is the most prone to leave his work to join in. Whenever there is activity around him, he is drawn to it. If there is no activity, he generates some.

These youngsters are also prone to talk out in class, at times to the point of seeming unable to refrain from talking. At times they act "clownish," and produce a response from the teacher because they have broken classroom rules. Such rules are most often those which demand quiet and physical inactivity in the classroom, rules difficult for the restless and socially active child to adhere to, even though he may obey other classroom guidelines (e.g., he will listen to all of the instructions before beginning work). The apparent lack of concern for rules and for the "rights" of others implicit in this intrusiveness is often a distressing factor for teachers who feel they must protect others from "negative" influences. Few teachers find it possible to ignore intrusive activity indefinitely, even if the child is in all other ways likeable.

Attraction to and causing noise and movement, even when annoying to others, must not be seen as having hostile intent. While many angry and hostile youngsters exhibit restlessness and cause disturbance, active and disturbing behavior is not necessarily the expression of hostility and anger. The child involved in the furor may be full of "fun" when active, and sincerely regretful if his activity hurts anyone else.

Restless behavior does not reflect a general trait of impulsiveness. The tendency toward physical movement and active social involvement with others through body contact or talk is not the same as impatience. The restless child does not necessarily fly off the handle with poorly controlled feelings. These tendencies may coexist in the same child, but one tendency may be manifest without the other.

Restless, active behavior is an intrinsic part of the makeup of some children from the very earliest ages. These youngsters naturally create and seek out social interaction, noise and "horsing around." They may act the clown, talk endlessly, and seem unable to sit still for a minute. Some are likeable, others are not; some angry and hostile, others are not; some very bright, others are not; some manifest other behaviors inconsistent with classroom learning, others do not.

How these behaviors affect adjustment and learning usually reflects how adults have responded to them. However, by themselves these behaviors do not suggest a disruption in the student-teacher relationship. Seldom do they alone arouse a deep negative feeling in the teacher. Nevertheless, what is crucial is that such behaviors often interfere with learning in the classroom, and demand that the teacher be sensitive to their occurrence and ready to respond constructively.

Alternative Teaching Strategies

Youngsters displaying restless, socially overactive and noise-making behavior have been the focus of the greatest number of studies concerned with effective teaching strategies. This is because such behaviors occur frequently, are easily observable, and are more apt to break the trend of classroom events than are other achievement-impeding behaviors. Teachers feel compelled, often realistically so, to respond in a way that will control the active child's behavior for him.

When planning for such a child in the learning environment it is important to keep in mind: (1) the youngster's high level of need for both social interaction and physical activity; (2) the importance of the surrounding interpersonal circumstances in stimulating, setting off and maintaining these behaviors; and (3) the apparent "thoughtless" quality of these actions. Each of these elements suggests alternative teaching strategies which might be used alone or in concert.

Legitimizing energy release

Because a youngster's active, restless behaviors often get out of control and disturb others, the youngster is often labeled a disrupter and suffers a variety of social punishments. The teacher's tendency is to react directly to these behaviors as the source of disruption and to subdue the youngster. Once he is subdued and the offending behavior arrested, the matter is mistakenly considered closed.

The youngster is expected subsequently to change his own behavior. If he does not, he is considered to have a problem, or is punished for continued misbehavior. Such approaches are rarely effective in aiding the restless and disturbing child.

Ignoring. As an initial approach the teacher may decide that he will not react at all, or at least not too quickly. By openly permitting activity "we sometimes really stop it faster than by any other technique."[1] If the disturbing behavior does not stop entirely, it may decrease to the point where it is no longer a problem, thus lessening the chance of conflict between teacher and child. "Planned ignoring," or allowing disturbing behaviors to continue, may be an effective alternative as long as the behavior is "within the range of tolerability"; that is, if disruptive behavior is "halfway kept in check, 'ignoring' leads to faster stoppage, at less expense than interference would."[2] This is true particularly if, in addition to the release of energy, the behaviors have taken on a secondary attention-getting function for the child, so that a reaction of almost any sort may only encourage more behavior of this nature in the future. By planning to ignore certain behaviors, the teacher can find out how much this overactive restlessness really needs to be dealt with directly and immediately. At the same time the youngster can learn that he will not gain the teacher's attention by such behavior. Furthermore, the teacher's too-quick intervention does not allow the child the time to attempt to settle himself down, and thereby takes away a chance for him to learn that he can and should contain himself. If the child does monitor his own behavior, the teacher must respond to it favorably and regularly, so that the child receives recognition for his growing self-control. If the child does not seem to be able to change, then alternative approaches should be considered.

Physical activity. Another useful approach requires that the teacher go beyond the immediate situation and capitalize upon the child's need for physical activity. Techniques which take into account the youngster's need to move about and to make noise, while at the same time teaching him something of educational value, turn otherwise disruptive behavior into a legitimate learning experience.

The teacher may do this by deliberately planning activities which require action. These activities might include songs, skits or stories that involve moving around and noise-making. The point is not simply to allow active free play. Free play may be useful to provide energy release for some youngsters. However, it is important to provide action games with some structure and rules to follow so that the child can learn that being active can be "good" and that there are times when it is not only acceptable but appropriate.

Planning ways to permit legitimate noisemaking and movement in the traditional classroom often takes ingenuity on the part of the teacher. It is also necessary, regardless of the type of classroom environment, to lay the groundwork by explaining the approach beforehand to other teachers and the principal. This is advisable because it is the rare school where, even for brief periods of time, yelling and clapping are legitimate activities. This constraint often causes a teacher to squelch a child even when he might feel that planned ignoring could be more educationally sound in the long run. Nonetheless, a brief noise and activity session once in a while in the classroom may be all an overactive child needs to enable him to function effectively as a student for the rest of the time. An example of such an approach was provided by one teacher who made noisemaking and physical activity a legitimate and educationally productive experience:

"As a preventive technique, I often make a game out of noisemaking when the group begins to get out of hand. 'Everyone stand up, stretch, and scream as loud as you can. What other ways can you make noise? Think of five different ways to make noise.' They really have to think, to come up with an unusual noise. I also tape record some of the noises and let the children try to identify them. The rest of the children close their eyes while the child goes to another part of the room and makes a noise, and the others guess what the noise is and where it came from. They have to think to come up with some noise that hasn't been done yet."

This type of activity not only legitimizes action and noisemaking but also alerts the child to the idea that he must be still and listen as well as be active and make noise. It allows the teacher to plan ahead by recognizing the needs of such youngsters, and is an approach which can be integrated into the learning process. It is important to recognize that the aim is not to stop activity, even overactivity, from ever occurring, but rather to make it part of legitimate, structured educational experiences. This decreases the tendency for the youngster to see himself as "bad" because he is restless and has disturbed others.

For youngsters too old for the type of game described above, the same principles still apply. For example, a child whose behavior is characterized by getting out of his seat, hitting others, being silly and making his classmates laugh, can be allowed a specific time to tell three jokes to the class. He is allowed to tell the jokes only if he refrains from disruptive, silly behavior for a specific period of time prior to this. To indicate to this youngster and to the rest of the class that there is a legitimate time for him to clown, the children can be told to ignore him and not laugh at him except during his joke period. This procedure can be coupled with other approaches which establish that there is a proper time for such activity and that when rules are broken, there will be consequences.[3] Although the particular strategy will of course vary, the essential quality of the approach remains: the activity is best when it provides energy release within the structure and plans of the educational program.

Providing constructive activities around the classroom routine. The goal of legitimizing energy release may also be accomplished with a variety of planned strategies using the regular work and chores of the classroom. The active child often welcomes being given helping jobs. At the first sign of disruption the youngster may be asked to help the teacher with a project. A youngster may be given some small responsibility in the classroom which allows him to move about in a productive way: cleaning a fishtank, emptying wastebaskets, erasing the blackboard. Errands frequently have to be run to other rooms, and these may be productively used when the child begins to get restless. Disruptive, restless behavior can often be alleviated by planning to provide constructive activities without resorting to attempts to directly suppress the behavior. By legitimizing the activity the teacher maintains a positive relationship with the child. The child finds rewards in productive activity, and eventually may seek such legitimate vehicles when he feels the need for activity and social stimulation.

Clarifying and articulating the issues

Ignoring disruptive behavior or allowing legitimate energy release will not always be sufficient. Many highly active and socially disruptive children do not realize what they are doing and its impact on others. Nor do they understand that some behaviors are acceptable and some are not. They may not be clear about the "rules of the game" that relate to demands for quiet, stillness, or respect for the privacy of others. Therefore, the teacher must be able to communicate clearly a reasonable behavioral standard as well as the reasons for this standard (e.g., everyone's right to privacy, the necessity to listen as well as to talk, the concept of fairness to others). Without such clarity the teacher appears arbitrary and unfair. The younger or more intellectually limited the child, the more concrete the teacher must be in describing what he expects as appropriate classroom behavior. When in doubt, the teacher should err by being overspecific in describing to children the standards of classroom conduct relating to disruptive behaviors.

Disruptive behavior often reflects the fact that teachers or other adults have responded in an inconsistent or uninterested way, or not at all, when a youngster has been "good." Also, the teacher's forced attention to the child when he is restless or disruptive amounts to an "overwhelming reinforcement of negative behavior."[4] Inconsistent and negative responses can seriously aggravate the problem, even given the teacher's best intentions to give positive attention to desired behaviors.

Personal discussions. One step to clarify the issues surrounding restless, disruptive behavior is a personal meeting with the youngster. It creates an opportunity to explore the youngster's awareness of his behavior and its consequences, his notions of why he acts as he does, and what he thinks the teacher expects of him.

One teacher explained the approach in this way: "Children may or may not realize they are doing the wrong thing, but because of our response or lack of it, don't know just quite what we expect of them. Teachers often have different expectations and this can be confusing. I try to explore reasons for his restlessness. What in your eyes is 'wrong' in his eyes may be perfectly fine. You must come to a meeting of the minds. I don't presume the child knows what I want and why I want it until I tell him. I say, 'You can come this far, but you'll step on my feet and disturb other people when you go beyond the limits.' I give examples of things he does that go over the limit and let him know what is expected and what isn't. I encourage him to talk about the limits so that I'm sure he understands them."

Such discussion is most productive when held at a time when there is no conflict and tension around his actions. To foster the child's thinking, direct questions may be asked in a personalized and nonjudgmental way: "I am wondering why you think you tease Elizabeth?" or "I notice you get very restless when you are with Alan. Could it be that you stir each other up a little too much? Perhaps you should sit apart until you finish your work and then sit with him."

These discussions often clarify the situation for the youngster, and the youngster often clarifies the situation for the teacher. The student has an opportunity to relate his behavior to circumstances as he sees them. The teacher offers similar information from his view of the youngster and his behavior. The purpose is not necessarily to come to a quick resolution about motives, but rather to afford an opportunity to understand each others' perceptions, the reasons for them, and how they have influenced behavior.

Following a discussion with the youngster, the teacher may recognize that a more specific teaching approach is needed if the youngster is to learn how to behave in the classroom.

"Mediation essays." Some children cannot talk clearly about their own problems or effective behaviors, and can provide only "sketchy and inaccurate" verbal pictures of what the rewards or punishments are for their behaviors. To foster such a youngster's ability to think "before, while, and after acting," the child can be given a typed copy of a paragraph describing the misbehavior, the desired behavior, and the consequences of both. He should practice and learn the paragraph by copying, paraphrasing, and reciting it orally. Then he should act out the disruptive behaviors described and the contrasting appropriate behaviors while reading the consequences to each aloud. These "mediation essays" may be created for any disruptive child along the following lines:

Each mediation essay contains four questions and their answers. The first question might be, "What did I do wrong?" which is followed by a sentence describing the child's misbehavior; for example, "I was walking around and making noise." The second question asks why the behavior is inappropriate; for example, "Why should I not walk around whenever I want to?" This question is followed by a statement describing vividly and in the child's vocabulary the consequences of this behavior: "If I disrupt the class by making noise, I may have to stay after school or write an essay about my behavior. Also, while not paying attention I am missing important work. Then I will not be able to understand what the class is doing and the class will be dull and boring. Time will drag slowly for me while others will find the assignments interesting." The third question focuses upon what the child should have been doing, followed by a brief but concrete description of the desired behavior: "I should walk across the room quietly, keeping my mouth closed and not touching others who are working." The fourth and last question concerns the reasons for the desired behavior; for example, "Why should I stay in my seat, or walk quietly?" This question is followed by a precise description of what the positive response from the teacher and class will be if the child displays those behaviors described as "what I should be doing." These descriptions should contain references to the tempting situations: "Even if I have a very interesting idea, I should get permission before speaking. Then the teacher and my classmates will be more likely to listen to what I have to say."[5]

Thus, if the child's picture of appropriate and inappropriate behavior and the consequences of these behaviors are unclear (and this is often the case), the child is given the means to think about and put into his own words what is expected. The teacher must not assume that merely telling the child about his misbehavior is enough to change it. Such an assumption often only leads to failure for the child and disappointment and frustration for the teacher.[6]

Signaling

The teacher may judge that on particular occasions immediate and direct action is needed to head off major disruption, and must use himself and the physical circumstances toward this end. In doing this it is helpful to know what physical and interpersonal arrangements in the classroom are important in generating and/or maintaining restless and disturbing activity, and which if changed, may alter this behavior.

One useful intervention is a simple, direct, attention-getting action or word from teacher to child. Such approaches have been labeled "signal interference."[7] A great deal of disruptive behavior occurs when a child "has been waylaid or swept aside" by a stimulating activity going on around him. If the teacher is able to catch a child's attention with a signal *before* the disruptive actions get out of hand, it is often possible to halt or redirect the behavior without further fanfare. These signals may be as straightforward as calling the child by name, or asking him to stop what he is doing. Some teachers find that all that is needed is a hard stare.[8] Others find it useful to discontinue teaching while noisemaking is occurring, thus demonstrating to the youngster that they are tuned in to what is going on in the classroom and have the legendary eyes in the back of their heads. To be effective, this intervention must stop the child early rather than after contagion has set in and others are involved, or the disruptive behavior has grown excessive. The teacher should be careful not to make the mistake of stopping a minor display of misbehavior which catches his eye, when a more serious one is taking place; for example, scolding a child for whispering when two other children are chasing each other around the room.[9]

These direct intervention methods are not intended as punishments and should not call attention to the child in such a way as to embarrass or create hurt feelings. They are intended to be external signals to indicate to the youngster that his behavior is getting out of hand. In some cases, it is useful to work out specific and even private signals with a youngster so that they become part of a verbalized agreement between teacher and child:

"When I stop teaching and wait, it will be a signal. Do you think that it is a good signal to remind you that you are making too much noise? Let's see if it will work." A few "practice" sessions during the same day as this discussion will help the child become more alert to that signal. The teacher might indicate, "I will be trying out our signal today by using it when you won't expect it. Let's see if you can catch me signaling you. Remember, I will stop talking and wait when you are making noise (or moving about, etc.)." The teacher might then carry out the procedure and at the same time catch the child's eye and smile or nod with approval as if to say, "You caught me using our signal. You remembered and I'm pleased."

At times open discussions with the entire class about the teacher's signaling behaviors aid all of the children to understand them as well as help a specific youngster to respond to them. The teacher might indicate that "sometimes some children need to be reminded that they are getting too noisy or moving around too much. I am going to use a signal to let them know that it is time to stop. If I do that, you will know that someone needs some help and you should keep working quietly in your place too. We will do this because noise and moving around sometimes interferes with others' work." The signal must be explained carefully so everyone understands and will recognize it. This involvement of the group is often useful because the development of acceptable behavior often follows the creation of socially shared values, and is maintained for many youngsters who disturb others by the need to interact and to meet peer standards.

Selective use of attention

If the teacher finds that attention-getting is the purpose of the disruptive behavior, and thus that teacher or peer attention is sustaining, not stopping the disruptive behavior, it is often helpful to discuss this first with the child alone. If the child denies that his motive is to gain the teacher's or peers' attention, the teacher can say that perhaps he (the teacher) is wrong, but that in any case he would always want to pay attention to a student who wants it. All the student need do is let him know *directly* by raising his hand or looking at the teacher. The teacher can agree that "if you want me to look at you, just look up to me and I'll look back, or come to your desk. But if you keep on acting up and making noise just because other children are paying attention to you, you will have to sit by yourself or leave the room. I will not give you attention if you misbehave."

An effective teaching technique is the combination of planned ignoring of disruptive behavior and selective attention to appropriate behavior. When a child is studying or participating in a class activity when requested to do so, the teacher should respond verbally (e.g., "Very good work" or

"I see you are studying"), move closer to the child, or give him a pat on the back. Teacher attention, signals or warnings for non-study and disruptive behaviors could be discontinued.[10]

If a child does not readily carry out requested classroom activities, but continues to be disruptive, the teacher can pay especial attention to each of the child's behaviors that contribute to appropriate studying, but that still fall short of the goal. Thus, even when the child merely takes out a pencil or paper or opens a book to the correct page, whether or not work is done, the teacher should provide a pleasant response. If disruptive behavior continues (for instance, the child frequently goes to the teacher to have work checked or to ask questions), then the teacher should ignore the child during this behavior but attend to him whenever he raises his hand while seated. Using this combination of responding to appropriate behaviors and ignoring those that are inappropriate, the teacher can bring about behavioral changes as well as increased academic achievement.

Reprimand and punishment

In addition to attending to appropriate behavior, the effect of planned reprimands and punishment as a means of intervention to decrease disruptive behavior should be considered. A number of studies have explored the effectiveness of using reprimands and punishment.

Working with a youngster who bothered others, argued and avoided any challenge to his behavior, and a second child who was uncooperative, giggled and said things aloud, the teacher was instructed to make all reprimands soft and personalized "so that only the child being reprimanded can hear you." This procedure was tested against the usual loud reprimands. It was reported that both children "displayed a marked reaction to soft reprimands," with a significant decrease in the disruptive behaviors. It was also noted that when the teacher used soft reprimands, he used fewer of them and gained better results than with the loud reprimands. In a second experiment with four other disruptive children, there was an increase in the disruptive behavior when loud reprimand was used following a period of soft reprimand. Examining the results, the authors suggested that when working with behaviorally disruptive children, an ideal combination of teaching techniques would probably be frequent praise, some soft reprimands, and very occasionally loud reprimands.[11]

Several experiments with behaviorally disturbed children have tested the use of mild punishment. The procedure used with one child involved merely giving him five colored strips of paper with his name on them at the beginning of each reading (and later arithmetic) period. He was told that the teacher was going to take a slip away each time he made noise during class. In both reading and arithmetic classes his misbehavior decreased markedly and almost immediately.

In a second classroom, ten of the boys "roamed around the room" and disrupted academic performance. The teacher placed a mark next to a child's name on a paper attached to a clipboard whenever the child left his seat. Each child was told to stay after school for five minutes for each time he was out of his seat. The out-of-seat behavior decreased under this condition but tended to return to former levels whenever the procedure was eliminated. Nonetheless, when used, mild punishment procedures did decrease the troublesome, achievement-retarding behaviors. In support of these techniques the authors noted that the mild punishment procedures used did not result in strong emotional responses and that they were effective with individuals and an entire class, at both elementary and high school levels.[12]

It has been recommended that punishment be utilized when it is ". . . a planful attempt by the adult to influence either the behavior or the long range development of a child or a group of children, for their own benefit, by exposing them to an unpleasant experience." Punishment should be designed to ". . . help the child get the taste of some consequences of his behavior and at the same time offer him a way to do something about it. . . ."[13]

*Using physical placement
in the classroom*

Changing the physical ecology of the classroom often helps in dealing with overactive and disruptive behaviors. External structure and supports to the child can be enhanced by seating him near the front of the room rather than its center. This strengthens the teacher's ability to control by being physically closer to the child and decreases peer support of the child's disruptive behavior. The teacher can use his own controlling presence by moving about the room as needed. Overactive behaviors diminish when the youngster sits next to and/or works with classmates who are not overactive and will not readily enter into disruptive behavior with him. Youngsters who are seldom drawn into such behavior do not stimulate it in the overactive youngster.

Selective rewarding procedures. When two disruptive children are seated next to each other, the teacher can effectively decrease the maladaptive behavior of both by carrying out selective rewarding procedures. One child is praised consistently for appropriate, non-disruptive behaviors, such as writing when it is assigned, looking toward the correct page, or looking at the teacher when he is talking. Misbehaviors are consistently ignored. The second child is provided no special response. Disruptive behaviors generally decrease and achievement-facilitating behaviors increase for both the child receiving the teacher's attention and the other child who is the observer, although more so for the child who is the focus of the teacher's attention.[14] This vicarious effect probably occurs often in the classroom, when children are close and can identify with one another's experiences.

Isolation. Another strategy to consider is that of isolating the restless, disturbing youngster, at least temporarily, from the others. The youngster may need to be given something to do by himself in a place where social stimulation is low. At times being at a desk or table by himself achieves this, especially when he is given a high-interest task to work on. These periods should be brief, with return to normal interaction with classmates as soon as the child seems ready. The teacher should always explain to the child that the purpose is to help him, for instance, to focus on his work or calm down, and not to punish him. If the behavior has reached the stage where self-control becomes impossible, then it may be necessary to utilize a planned time out as described in Chapter 8, Coping with Negative Feelings and Actions. This is particularly so if the attention of peers is causing the child to continue his disruptive behavior.

Capitalizing upon
social motivation

The interpersonal drive frequently found in such youngsters may also be capitalized upon in productive ways. The reward these youngsters are willing to work for often involves the opportunity for interaction.

Tutoring fellow classmates. If the youngster has finished some assigned work or has displayed effort to keep from disrupting others, he may be allowed to help someone else. Tutoring a fellow classmate in one of his stronger subjects channels this child's social drive into helping rather than hindering. Through such opportunities he gains the respect of peers and enhances positive feelings from the teacher. He can change his image from that of "the kid who always stops other kids from working" to that of someone who helps others. Children do have such images of themselves and of their classmates, and these images do relate to a child's success in the classroom.[15]

Even the more limited student can be drawn into a tutor role to provide him with the opportunity to interact productively. For example, the child who can spell eight words may tutor the child who knows two words. They can then work together to learn other words. Student-to-student tutoring is a useful and effective procedure since it not only meets the youngster's need to interact but also provides the opportunity to practice classroom material by teaching someone else. Furthermore, the child's productive, non-disturbing behaviors in the tutoring interaction afford the teacher the opportunity to express enthusiasm about his performance: "How well you two worked together without noise" or "You helped Fred so much." If disturbing behaviors occur during tutoring, the teacher can use more direct intervention approaches as described in the following sections.

Outside activities. Among older youngsters the context of social interaction may also include club activity, project construction, collections of trip money, and the variety of social activities surrounding school life but not always capitalized upon during the regular school day. They also include, for example, choral reading and acting out scenes from reading material. These activities are often reserved for special events; however, for the youngster who needs to be involved with others, they are most helpful because they give him a reason for practicing and working at the tasks—the opportunity to interact with peers.

Group discussions. It is important to emphasize that activity level and social interaction, particularly among older youngsters, need not be viewed only at the gross motor level (i.e., merely running or shouting). Engagement of the youngster in verbal interaction becomes a functional equivalent. One strategy, for instance, is to make a point to encourage the youngster to express his opinion as frequently as possible, or in other ways provide him many opportunities to participate in an ongoing discussion with the group. Since they are talkers anyway, why not capitalize upon this drive? Depending upon other abilities, it is sometimes useful to use debate or a radio or TV broadcast, or some equivalent challenging form of verbal interaction as a means for the youngster to productively release his energies and yet continue to work with the group. Once a child has learned to use his own "mediation essay" (described earlier in this chapter), he may be able to help another learn from that youngster's set of essays.

It is possible to further capitalize upon the drive toward interaction by holding group discussions that focus upon common needs; for example, "We need to be able to work together successfully." Such discussions afford the teacher an opportunity to discuss the purpose of laws or rules, the rights people have as individuals, and the needed balance between personal rights and social obligations. Developmentally, elementary school youngsters are concerned about and ready to grasp these concepts. They are often quick to express their notions of fairness, the behaviors of peers that are annoying or intrude upon them, and what they feel should be the rules about these matters in the classroom. Depending upon the age of the youngsters, these may even be written down and posted as existing "laws" of a classroom society. This need not be a list of platitudes or merely a list of "don'ts." Acceptable as well as unacceptable behaviors should be discussed, written down, and discussed again in concrete terms.

Peer involvement. The important issue is that whatever the rules, the teacher must let the students know they have the right as a social group to play a significant part in establishing and carrying them out. On this point the evidence is clear: jointly established rules have far greater chance for success than those imposed by the teacher; and following the establishment of socially held rules, the disruptive youngster's classmates are more willing and able to help him follow "our rules." In fact, peer reaction to transgression of these class rules may better serve as a corrective experience than any teacher response. Usually these youngsters are more apt to appreciate a negative reaction on the part of a peer than the teacher. As noted earlier, the overactive youngster is socially oriented, and does not like being rejected. At times he may not understand why a classmate is angry with him. The teacher may use such occasions to explain to the youngster why he got a hostile reception. Getting such a reaction helps him appreciate that he cannot interrupt or tease someone else whenever he wants to, and that he cannot ignore the fact that others have a right to do what they want without intrusion. The teacher can help a youngster make this connection, but often only after he has experienced the negative reaction of a classmate.

The teacher should be alert to the fact that approaches which capitalize upon the need for social interaction may serve to increase the problem if care is not taken. Often misbehavior is maintained, not decreased, by peer attention. An intervention approach should be designed to involve peers productively, as in the following example. Popular students were selected and trained to help disruptive peers improve their behavior. The popular peers were asked if they would help others to improve their behavior because it was "a cause of their poor school performance." They were told to try to ignore any disruptive behavior and to respond positively to desirable behaviors. Each of these behaviors was specified (e.g., When the classmate is out of his seat without permission this is disruptive, and when he asks permission this is desirable). Each time they noticed the disruptive fellow student engaging in non-disruptive work behavior, they were to pay attention to him and mark a "+" on a rating chart. If they inadvertently noticed and reacted to the child when he was engaging in one of the specified disruptive behaviors, they were to mark a "-" on the chart. At the end of the day the teacher discussed the ratings to emphasize that they were to ignore disruptive behaviors and only look at the child when he was working appropriately.

The peers initially attended to and maintained the disruptive, deviant behaviors at a "somewhat alarming" rate. However, following training the major shift of the peers' attention was away from responding to disruptive behavior as well as (although less than) toward responding to the display of appropriate behavior. When this occurred, disruptive behaviors decreased and productive behaviors increased. Under the direction of the teacher, peers can be taught to be involved in aiding their more troubled classmates, and can serve as a great help to the teacher as well as the disruptive child.[16]

Aiding the student
to monitor his own behavior

Once the issue of disturbing vs. appropriate behavior has been clarified, either through discussion or direct intervention or both, the teacher might still find it necessary to have the child keep track of his own behavior. Such an approach has been described earlier as being effective in helping the inattentive child because the teacher shares the responsibility for behavior control with the child. For the disruptive child the teacher may indicate that he believes the student should "signal" his own behavior by recording, each time he is reminded by the teacher, that he is out of his seat, annoying others or making noise. Some youngsters may even be able to monitor their own behavior without notification from the teacher. They can indicate each time they realize that they are annoying another child or making noise, as well as each time they are aware of the fact that they are working well.

This technique has been used successfully with a boy who was out of his seat so frequently that he distracted everyone. His behavior was so seriously maladaptive that, following referral for psychiatric services, recommendation was made for residential treatment and psychotherapy. Prior to institution of these recommendations, a special plan was developed as a last effort to maintain the child in a regular class. Since getting out of his seat was the single most disruptive behavior, this was pointed out to the child. He was given a chart on which he was to mark each time he was out of his seat. During the first two weeks the boy threw the chart away and resisted keeping a record of his behavior. However, the chart was given back to him each time and by the third week he agreed to keep it and mark his behavior. The act of self-recording and improvement in behavior were responded to in a rewarding manner by the teacher. The child's out-of-seat behaviors stopped completely, and referral and removal from the classroom were no longer judged necessary.[17]

A self-recording procedure has also been used with students who talk out excessively. An eighth-grade boy who repeatedly disturbed the class by talking out was given a slip of paper and instructed to "record a mark every time you talk out without permission." No other instructions were given. The self-recording was collected at the end of each class period and discussed. The teacher praised the child for whatever progress he made. In spite of this boy's expressed lack of desire to change and his initial refusal to use the self-recording procedure, there was significant progress in the direction of more effective behavior.[18]

Contracting

Another approach, which combines several already described, involves reaching a formalized agreement with the student. The teacher may suggest privately that the youngster and he enter into a "contract." The teacher and child then spell out the exact disruptive behaviors that are to be changed, the agreed-upon standards of good conduct and the consequences to follow upon "good" and "bad" behaviors. For example, a contract might state:

"No one is to interrupt the work of another student. We agree that the student must talk in a whisper during the time when others are reading or working. If the student works quietly during the quiet work time, extra time will be earned to do something he wants to do. The teacher will remind him only once that he is being noisy. If he does not come quickly back to his work after one signal from the teacher, he will receive a black mark and have to sit by himself. If he does not disturb others for a specific period of time, he will be rewarded by being able to do something he likes."

The contract should call for and reward accomplishment rather than obedience. Thus, rather than stating to the child, "If you do what I tell you to do, I will reward you by...," the teacher should indicate, "If you accomplish the goal of..., you will be rewarded by...." To be fair, the reward must be something the child values and should be of "equal weight" to the behavioral demands. The equality of value between task and reward might best be judged following discussion between teacher and child. It is clear, however, that five minutes of quiet work should not be rewarded with two hours of free play, and neither should the reward be so small or put off into the future that it takes on little motivational meaning. Some investigators have suggested that work and play be alternated in equal time lots. Others have found that a very small reward (e.g., an inexpensive toy) will be sufficient to sustain a contract for good behavior for an entire class period. In any case, the agreement should present reasonable demands and provide reasonable rewards.[19]

Summary

This behavior dimension is comprised of behaviors that interrupt a productive flow of learning. They indicate a turning away from a work task and toward activities that impede learning. For example, what begins as a shared project with a microscope becomes a situation where one youngster taunts another about his haircut, hides his slides, or in some other way diverts his attention from a learning task. This may occur quietly, although usually noise emerges sooner or later. The noise level, however, is not a reliable criterion of the presence of restless, disturbing, achievement-impeding behaviors. A classroom may be filled with the productive noise of children moving about, debating what ought to be done on a project, laughing with excitement or surprise, and in general sharing thoughts in open conversation.

Most important to those concerned with aiding children who display disruptive, restless behaviors is that (as is the case with children who display negative feelings and actions) these behaviors relate to academic failure *less* in classes where activity is not only allowed but is also an encouraged part of the learning process. While restless, disturbing behaviors occur in all types of classes, those classrooms where student activity and verbal responsiveness are made an integral part of the learning process allow these behaviors to occur without

180

necessarily impeding the students' academic progress. [20] Thus, for example, if a classroom is arranged so that a student does not have to sit in his seat to do classwork, moving about is not necessarily a disruption of the learning process and social engagement may not be irrelevant to learning. If activity level does interfere with learning, academic success for these youngsters is fostered by a combination of clearly established guidelines; external cues or signals for aiding self-control; and teaching strategies that channel or redirect, rather than suppress, energy release and social interaction. Teaching strategies that channel or redirect energy are more effective when they are applied at the first signs of impending disruption. Catching things before they exceed acceptable limits eliminates the need for negative emotions and shifts behavior before the youngster becomes overinvolved in responding to the negative reactions he generates from others.

In all the strategies involving manipulation of the physical and social ecology of the classroom, it is important to keep in mind that the main issue is intervention to supplement the youngster's self-control; it is not punishment. These youngsters are generally socially oriented, and prolonged social isolation will only become punishment rather than an assistance to the youngster in learning to bring his behavior to acceptable levels. Teaching approaches "should contribute something to the child's experience, rather than take something away from him."[21] The object of each of these approaches is not to reduce self-esteem, but to foster the child's development of self-control. Many strategies require manipulation of social forces and the creation of consequences for the child. They are more apt to have lasting effects when they include concern for ways to aid the child to develop the "inner," self-regulating processes of understanding, anticipation, and problem-solving that ultimately will allow him to control his own behavior.

Footnotes

[1] F. Redl and D. Wineman. *Controls from within.* Glencoe: The Free Press, 1952, p. 218.

[2] Ibid., p. 159.

[3] D. J. Dickinson. Changing behavior with behavioral techniques. *Journal of School Psychology,* 1968, *6,* 278-283.

[4] W. A. McClain. The modification of aggressive classroom behavior through reinforcement, inhibition, and relationship therapy. *Training School Bulletin,* 1969, *65,* 122-125.

[5] R. O. Blackwood. The operant conditioning of verbally mediated self-control in the classroom. *Journal of School Psychology,* 1970, *8,* 251-258.

[6] Ibid.

[7] Redl and Wineman, p. 160.

[8] Ibid., pp. 160-163

[9] J. S. Kounin and S. Obradovic. Managing emotionally disturbed children in regular classrooms: A replication and extension. *The Journal of Special Education,* 1968, *2,* 129-135.

[10] R. V. Hall, D. Lund and D. Jackson. Effects of teacher attention on study behavior. *Journal of Applied Behavior Analysis,* 1968, *1,* 1-12.

[11] K. D. O'Leary, K. F. Kaufman, R. E. Kass and R. S. Drabman. The effects of loud and soft reprimands on the behavior of disruptive students. *Exceptional Children,* 1970, *37,* 145-155.

[12] R. V. Hall, S. Axelrod, M. Foundopoulos, J. Shellman, R. A. Campbell and S. S. Cranston. The effective use of punishment to modify behavior in the classroom. In K. D. O'Leary and S. G. O'Leary (Eds.), *Classroom management: The successful use of behavior modification.* New York: Pergamon Press, Inc., 1972, pp. 173-182.

[13] F. Redl. The concept of punishment. In N. J. Long, W. C. Morse and R. G. Newman (Eds.), *Conflict in the classroom.* Belmont, California: Wadsworth Publishing Company, Inc., 1965, pp. 345-352.

[14] M. Broden, C. Bruce, M. A. Mitchell, V. Carter and R. V. Hall. Effects of teacher attention on attending behavior of two boys of adjacent desks. *Journal of Applied Behavior Analysis,* 1971, *4,* 191-199.

[15] E. M. Bower. *Early identification of emotionally handicapped children in school.* Springfield, Illinois: C. C. Thomas, 1969, pp. 63-67.

[16] R. W. Solomon and R. G. Wahler. Peer reinforcement control of classroom problem behavior. *Journal of Applied Behavior Analysis,* 1973, *6,* 49-56.

[17] R. Kroth. Behavior management techniques. Paper presented at Council for Exceptional Children, 46th International Conference, New York, 1968.

[18] Broden et al.

[19] L. Homme et al. *How to use contingency contracting in the classroom.* Champaign, Illinois: Research Press Co., 1970.

[20] G. Spivack and M. Swift. Behavioral adjustment in the open classroom. *International Journal of Applied Psychology,* in press.

[21] Homme et al., p. 20.

11 Fostering the Student's View That What He Does Makes a Difference

This behavior dimension reflects the youngster's tendency to see external circumstances as the cause of his difficulties. He expresses the idea that something is wrong outside of him when things are not going well, when he is confronted with something new, or when a task requires some effort or thought. The youngster complains that the teacher will not show him how to do things or will not answer his questions to his satisfaction. Thus, to a large extent he blames the teacher for his failures and frustrations. When he does poorly on a task or test, he is also likely to blame the test or surrounding circumstances. He may say the work was too hard, he wasn't given enough time, or that others were bothering him, adding (or at least implying) that the teacher is expecting too much.

This tendency to blame external circumstances may be rather subtle in older youngsters. For instance, the youngster may claim that he cannot do the work assigned because he is not capable enough. In such instances, when the teacher knows that he is capable and judges that he is underestimating himself, the implication is that the teacher is at fault. Again, the youngster feels that the teacher is expecting too much of him, thereby making his life an unhappy one. In extreme cases, the youngster may also complain that his peers are making fun of him and respond to them with open and hostile criticism.

This dimension taps the degree to which the youngster blames other persons or the environment when his self-esteem is threatened by failure or the prospect of failure. He feels that his difficulty is not self-determined or a reflection of his own deficiency in not studying enough or listening well enough in class. His problem resides in an overdemanding, unhelpful, or even neglectful environment, and he may demonstrate this by complaining that the teacher never calls on him or calls on others first. Whatever the discomfort, there is a need to see causality primarily as external: the teacher (and others) have let him down, leaving him helpless.

It is important to add that the tendency to blame circumstances is frequently manifest in young children, and is not always inappropriate. However, as children mature into later childhood and adolescence, this tendency should diminish, reflecting an increasing awareness and development of a "self," as well as a parallel increase in a sense of power over and competence in dealing with life and its problems. The youngster who continues to blame external circumstances has not developed the feeling that he has some control over what happens to him in the classroom.

When a youngster blames circumstances for his difficulties, he is not necessarily being hostile. There may be a hostile flavor, when the expression of blame is accompanied by the expression of anger and alienation from a student who feels powerless in what he views as a hostile world. On the other hand, his underlying feeling may be fear, helplessness, frustration or disappointment, and his blaming behavior may actually be a call for help. Even when the child exhibits other behavior problems, the importance of this blaming behavior is that it indicates the youngster does not see himself as the cause of his problems. For all school age youngsters, excessive display of external blaming indicates an inadequate response to classroom demands, and accompanies poor academic achievement.

Alternative Teaching Strategies

The core issues underlying external blaming behaviors are feelings of powerlessness in the classroom, low self-esteem concerning educational productivity, and an expectation of failure. These feelings are accompanied by the view that problems result from what the teacher does or does not do, and not from what the student does himself. The relationship between student and teacher, as viewed by the youngster, is that of an overwhelmed, unwanted, helpless child and an ignoring, insensitive, uninterested adult. This is so because the teacher is seen as determining all success and failure, good feelings as well as bad feelings. Given this point of view, it is reasonable that any failure or anticipated failure would lead the student to the conclusion that the teacher is not doing something he should be doing (e.g., helping the student), is doing something wrong (e.g., giving too much or too difficult work), or is not really interested in providing chances for the student to be successful (e.g., does not call on the student).

Checking the reality
of the student's claims

In view of the student's feelings about the "unfair" or "unreasonable" desires of the teacher, it is particularly necessary for the teacher to check the reality of the student's assertion that the blame for his difficulties is outside of himself. The teacher must be willing to reflect honestly upon and examine what he is asking the student to do. He must make sure that the work is at the appropriate level. Very often, for example, students are assigned books in a subject area without consideration of the readability level of the material, or are given instructions that are unclear. Many students report that they read material or instructions over and over again without really understanding what they have read or what they are to do. It is not surprising that many such students feel the teacher is at fault for their failures and frustrations. If the teacher finds that the level of assignment is too high or that the student's claim of not being helped enough is true, then certain remedial steps are warranted. First, a search must be made for more appropriate level material and an effort made to provide some additional time for that student. In such cases, a teacher who admits he may have expected too much or inadvertently ignored a youngster can turn matters around dramatically. The teacher can foster the view that he wants to help by showing rather than telling the child what to do. He can take time to encourage and answer the youngster's questions about the work. As pointed out in Chapter 9, Allaying Achievement Anxiety, asking questions about the work is often a sign of motivation, suggesting the child's own drive to achieve. Both teacher and student can change their views of one another if there is an effort to work together to eliminate the source of student concern. If, on the other hand, the teacher concludes that the student's external blaming is not warranted—the youngster is actually capable of performing at the level the teacher is demanding, and is getting reasonable support and help from him—other strategies must be employed.

"Reflex" responses teachers frequently make when confronted with a student whose blaming is unwarranted are usually counterproductive and thus should be avoided. One response is to assert flatly that, "You can do it if you only try." If the teacher is convinced that the student can do what is expected, a better response might be, "Sometimes we all think we can't do some things that we can do. I understand how you feel, but I know you are able to do it. You can try." In this instance, if the child does try, it is important for the teacher to indicate that he is pleased with the "try" and then to look for successful work that can be praised. The teacher might say in a joking and pleased way to the child alone, "You wanted me to think you couldn't do it, but you knew you could."

A second unproductive response to the child who claims that the teacher does not help or makes work too hard is to indicate that the youngster is being unreasonable, unappreciative, or just a chronic complainer. The blaming behaviors are, on the surface, critical of the teacher and suggest he is not doing his job. However, these behaviors actually reflect the student's lack of confidence in his ability and/or the feeling that "no one is going to make me do what I don't want to do." Whichever the case, counterattack or the threat that the student had better perform "or else" will not work. Although it might lead to some limited production at the moment, such a reaction strengthens the youngster's conception of the teacher as the all-powerful and insensitive determiner of what the youngster produces in class. Since this view is unrealistic, and interferes with learning and the student's relationship with the teacher, the teacher should do nothing to encourage it.

Further, there is a third type of response which is of limited value with these youngsters. Since much blaming behavior is a seeming call for help, the teacher might erroneously construe such behavior as meaning merely that the youngster is emotionally dependent and in need of more attention. Teachers often attempt to fill this need by calling on the student more, telling him he can have help whenever he wants it, offering tutoring, or designing make-up tests. Although the teacher may feel that this added attention will make the student feel more secure and thus less critical of others, it is often counterproductive since it reinforces the belief that the teacher can solve (or fail to solve) all problems. And the youngster's tendency to externalize causes for what happens often does not diminish. The more the teacher tries to help by manipulating the youngster's world and altering demands made upon him, the more the youngster seems to have difficulty learning to accept responsibility for coping with stressful academic situations on his own.

Appropriate teaching strategies must take into consideration the youngster's low self-esteem and feelings of inability to succeed on the basis of what *he* does. Arguing in defense of academic demands or becoming annoyed with the youngster will not help him; rather, the youngster may become anxious or angered, suffering an even lower sense of well-being in that classroom. Providing extra attention will also not aid this youngster; what he needs are experiences in which he can relate success to his own efforts.

*Discussing the youngster's feelings and
linking his efforts to his work*

To make academic success possible, the teacher can initially have a private talk with the youngster about his unhappy feelings. "I know at times you must feel unable to do the work. I guess that sometimes you wish I would make things easier so you could do it easily. Could it be that sometimes you are afraid to try because you don't think you can do it?" The teacher should communicate to the youngster, without embarrassing or punishing him, that his feelings are understood and acceptable. The teacher should not try to soften the feelings, or convince the youngster that he should not have these feelings (e.g., "But you mustn't feel that way" or "That's a silly way to feel because you can really do the work").

The issue is not the child's ability, but his lack of self-confidence in his own initiative and/or his conflict over doing work for the teacher. These students often feel, "I can never please this teacher." The teacher should indicate that the student can participate by explaining exactly what it is that he wants help with. "If you have a question from now on, you must ask about it"; or "I do not know what you are thinking, so you must tell me what you know and don't know"; or "If you are having difficulty understanding something, and you begin to worry or get upset, just raise your hand, and I will try to help you work on it"; or "I know that sometimes you get angry when you don't understand something because you are upset. That's all right. But don't forget that we can discuss what it is you are having difficulty with." In these discussions the emphasis should be upon what the student can do. Focusing upon a task that is "too hard," the teacher can ask, "What can you do with this assignment? If you did that, what will happen? You try and let's see." In addition to moving the student to take initiative, this approach also allows the teacher to see if the student does understand what he is supposed to do. If he does the work incorrectly, the teacher can indicate that he sees that things are going wrong. "How did you do this part. . . (indicating a part he did correctly)?" The teacher thereby demonstrates understanding of the student's plight, gives recognition that the student has been successful, and communicates his belief that the student is capable of taking some responsibility for his work.

In all of this, the teacher creates and maintains a role of helper and guide, not all-powerful knower, giver, and taker. The approach begins with recognizing and accepting feelings, and moves toward linking the student's thoughts and efforts to his work.

Recording success

One way to aid the student to view success as the result of his own work is to teach him to observe and record his successes. Each student should keep track only of his own work and no comparison should be made with others. The student can make up a series of graph pages on which he can mark the number of things he does right. If he says he could not do something because, for instance, the teacher did not help him enough, the teacher can ask if he still wishes to record what he did do on his success chart. In this way the focus is kept on what the youngster has done and his chart, rather than how these relate to the teacher. After a period of such recording, the teacher's response to such claims as, "I can't. It's too hard. You won't help me," can be "What does your success chart tell you you can do?" or "Why do you think you are saying it's too hard?" Systematic examination of the success chart can then be made and the discussion centered around what the student did to attain the success. While such a technique might be used routinely with most children, it is probably best to use it only with students for whom success is elusive. This approach can be counterproductive for successful students because it slows down their work and rate of progress.

Emphasizing student initiatives

Another useful strategy is to allow the student to be a decision-maker. One way to afford him the feeling that he has power over his destiny is to involve him in planning his educational program. If he raises a problem, the teacher might focus upon what plans the student may have to overcome it. He may ask the student to judge what it will take in time or effort to finish a task. The teacher can ask him in what different ways he could approach the problem or, if appropriate, offer a variety of alternatives for student consideration.

In all of this, the purpose is to encourage exploration and to support the youngster in making a decision for himself. The teacher must not decide, but rather should support the youngster's decision. This requires that there be some latitude in accepting his suggestions: "What choice would you prefer?" "Which of these three ways do you feel more comfortable using. . .?" "Can you choose something from the things we have to do?" "Which of these do you think you can do?"

The teacher can also allow the student to participate in evaluating his own work. Again, this procedure draws the student's own judgment into the open, even if it is initially unreasonable. In handling the student's self-appraisal, the teacher should minimize imparting his judgments because they quickly squelch the youngster's imparting his own. The teacher can, however, encourage the youngster to verbalize why he appraises a particular product as he does: "You have done most of the problems correctly. What do you think your grade should be?" or "I'm going to give you a paragraph with the ten words you had yesterday. Five are spelled wrong. How many of the five spelled wrong do you think you will find?" The latter response is an instance of having the youngster predict his own success, allowing for later focus upon how well he thinks he did and why.

It is always useful to relate what the youngster accomplishes to the work and effort he put into it. Whenever possible, it is good to highlight how some amount of preparation, previous study, paying attention, or other effort on the student's part resulted in a better end product. If he verbalizes a relationship between a particular success and some effort he previously put into his work, the teacher should provide a supporting comment: "Yes, you sure must have worked hard on that project. Your work shows it" or "I can tell you studied on your own." In the same context of fostering self-initiative and the feeling of self-confidence, if the student verbalizes "I don't understand" instead of "You don't help me enough, it's too hard," this too should be recognized and supported, for it is a sign of progress. The student is showing that he is seeing himself as a significant person in the learning process and as one who has a right to ask questions.

Summary

The focus when working with youngsters who externalize blame is on generating with them the feeling that they can control through knowledge, skill, or questions more of what happens to them in class than they may have thought, and that rewards (and failures) depend in large part upon what they do and do not do, rather than the exigencies of luck or the teacher's kindness. This kind of difficulty is often overlooked and there is a paucity of projects in this area reported in the research literature. Nonetheless, the evidence presented in Chapter 1 indicates that many children display behaviors suggesting that they feel powerless in the educational setting. Overcoming this belief is deemed crucial to academic success.

In the planning of approaches to foster the feeling that the student does have some control over what is happening to him, the teacher must first examine the nature of the demands made. Is the child accurate in his view that the teacher does not help him enough, does not call upon him, or has given him work which is too difficult? If any of these is the case, learning is impeded until the appropriate changes are made to indicate the teacher's recognition of the legitimacy of the child's criticisms. However important, this is often not sufficient. Many youngsters express these feelings even when careful observation indicates that the teacher is trying to help, does call on them, and is not giving work that is too difficult. Direct attempts to convince these youngsters that they can do the work are of little value in overcoming their doubts about classroom demands or their doubts about themselves and the teacher. The teacher only appears insensitive to them. Meeting their complaints merely by giving extra attention is not sufficient and offers only temporary relief. It may in the long run only further convince these youngsters that happiness and success, or frustration and failure, are caused by the teacher.

These youngsters must have many opportunities in which they can take initiative to solve their own problems. Learning becomes possible when work is planned with them and not solely for them. It is helpful to provide the child with his own concrete evidence of the success of his efforts. The topic of conversation between teacher and student can be on what the student did to gain success in his own work. The teacher can show his pleasure by indicating recognition of the child's efforts. The child should be encouraged to tell in his own words the steps he took to resolve a problem, thereby fostering the student's view of himself as competent. An equally important aim is to foster the view that the teacher is someone who is there to help him learn, not someone who causes his success. When this student learns he has control of his own successes and can verbalize how he achieved them, it is more probable that he can then develop a planful approach when he has been unsuccessful. Success is then within his power, and he is able to overcome failure or frustration rather than view them as evidence that the teacher has failed him again.

12 Common Elements in Teaching Strategies

The preceding chapters have outlined strategies a teacher should consider when confronted with children who have a variety of troubled behaviors. At times the strategies are presented with no specific sequencing or preference suggested; at other times, a specific sequencing is offered. If the teacher, or consultant to the teacher, wants to know what he might do in a particular instance, he can refer to the suggestions in the appropriate chapter. No generalization serves completely when one needs specific advice about dealing with a concrete problem.

When we step back from these specific chapters, however, we find certain common elements that generalize across many of the strategies for specific problem behaviors. Surveying these general strategies is useful for at least two reasons: first, an appreciation of a general strategy provides a guide to the many specific applications for a child with a particular set of difficulties; second, such general strategies often constitute an overall approach to all children, many of whom either already manifest achievement-impeding behaviors or will do so sometime during the school year.

General considerations

Before discussing these common elements, a few preliminary comments must be made which the teacher should keep in mind, regardless of the strategy used.

Change takes time

Whatever a teacher decides to do in relation to a specific child will probably take time. In consulting with teachers we have often heard them comment that they have tried everything and "nothing works." Under more careful scrutiny, however, it has usually been the case that no one plan of action had been devised and given time to succeed, even if a plan had shown promise. As adults we often try one thing after another with children, and when change does not occur quickly we throw up our hands in defeat.

To make maximum use of the ideas in this book for devising strategies to aid a child in the classroom, the teacher must remain aware that behavior change takes time. For example, if selective praise is the approach used with a child needing support and reassurance, it must be applied consistently over more than a few days before any results can occur. Furthermore, many plans require a stepwise progression over time, with recognition given to the fact that each separate step takes time in its own right. Other plans require that the teacher return to speak with a child or check his work the next day. In such instances the teacher must provide the child with a sense of continuity by planning a future meeting with him and then carrying it through. It has also been suggested in many cases that the teacher should act as a model for the child to imitate. For instance, when working with the impatient youngster, the teacher would constantly attempt to demonstrate reflective and patient behavior, which may very well involve changing his own habitual responses. In almost all cases, a plan can be more beneficial to a youngster if he is made aware by word or demonstration that it takes time before positive results will be felt. Whatever the details, however, the teacher must consider time as an ally—as a medium through which change will take place—and not a taskmaster and source of pressure.

What the teacher does
makes a difference

It is also necessary to realize and appreciate that the teacher cannot avoid responding to achievement-impeding behaviors. The only choice open to the teacher is whether or not he wishes to devise a plan beforehand. In some cases a child's behavior will demand that the teacher react because it creates a crisis in the classroom. In other instances, the behavior may be more benign and thus ignored or not even seen. However, even in the latter instance the teacher is affecting the behavior of the child, even though at the moment neither may be aware of it. What the teacher does by a momentary reaction encourages the child to continue or halt a particular action. For example, a quick reprimand may temporarily push it underground; ignoring or failing to notice it may cause the behavior to disappear. The point is that a teacher's behavior has an impact upon students' behavior, whether or not he wishes this to be the case, and he cannot avoid the responsibility implicit here.

The teacher is a significant element in the interpersonal ecology of the classroom, and as a result is continually making an impact upon the children in significant ways. We believe it is better that the teacher be aware of this fact and react or choose not to react according to a plan.

The teacher as an initiator

As the reader may have already noted, few of the strategies suggested in preceding chapters require that the teacher involve others outside of the classroom. Visiting and conferring with parents is suggested for dealing with problems of inattentive, negative and uninvolved children; in a few instances specific strategies are offered that would require the collaboration of other teachers or school personnel. However, we have attempted to suggest mainly strategies that are feasible for the teacher himself to employ in the classroom.

If the teacher wants to involve others in a plan for a child, whether the others are parents or teachers, it is the teacher who must assume initiative. Further, he must have a goal and plan of action in mind, or little of use will be accomplished. Perhaps in the best of all worlds we may conceive of settings where there are people and sufficient time available to discuss and share all our thoughts and problems. However, the usual work-a-day world of the teacher does not afford such luxuries. If there is to be a collaborative effort, the teacher must have a strategy designed to offer the other person, and hope to convince that person of its benefit for everyone involved.

Common elements of teaching strategies

One-to-one contact
between teacher and child

One element in the range of potential strategies for dealing with almost every behavior problem dimension is the personal contact between teacher and child. This fact in itself suggests that an important skill in teaching is the ability to relate on a personal basis with youngsters. With the inattentive child, the teacher tries to discover the reasons behind his boredom, fear, or preoccupation. The teacher may wish to establish rapport with the uninvolved or negative child, reach out to the child who is withdrawn, calm down the anxious child. It is in the private conversation between teacher and child that special, individual "signals" are agreed upon and contracts are concluded. It is the occasion to discover special interests, give special praise or attention, or share personal feelings.

There is no substitute for getting to know a child on an individual basis, particularly when planning for the children described in this book. The fact is that in most classrooms too much time is spent responding to problems that might have been alleviated by an effective interpersonal link between teacher and child. It is often extremely difficult to successfully reinvolve a child in classwork and other learning activities following a troublesome episode without some amount of personal discussion. Understanding and discussing unacceptable behavior is more apt to occur if contact and talk prior to the problem episode has taken place. Such talk need not take much time, and a busy schedule is no excuse if the teacher wishes to aid the children's learning. In some cases, the fact that a child has been singled out for a moment may be more important for him than the length of contact, and may be sufficient to enable teacher and child to work together in resolving difficulties. This personal touch is manifest in many simple ways: a wink, smile, gesture, or a brief whisper to the child as if to say, "I remember you're here and like you personally" or "Sorry I yelled yesterday—I was just upset about something else. I'm not mad at you now."

A few cautions must be kept in mind regarding one-to-one contacts with some children, lest the teacher feel an indiscriminate pressure for interaction that may actually be harmful in the long run. This is especially true when the child's problem behaviors involve a difficulty in relating to adults. For example, the child who is excessively anxious about performing and being correct usually views adults as standard-setters and critics. The teacher must realize that, at least initially, any request to talk with such a child may stimulate anxiety, overconcern, and an anticipation that he will be judged adversely. In early stages the learning situation must be interpersonally defused, and one way to do this is to impersonalize learning tasks in some respects (e.g., the teacher may not grade papers or may provide automated feedback curriculum materials).

A somewhat similar caution is warranted when a child exhibits overreliant behaviors. Since such a youngster is quick to look to the teacher for guidance and direction, care must be taken during any one-to-one interchange not to further stimulate this form of dependence. Such children almost reflexively seek cues outside of themselves as to what to do. In any private discussion the teacher must studiously avoid such a leadership role and support the child's own evolving inner-directedness by helping him to articulate and make choices for himself.

Another caution must be exercised with the child who blames externals (including the teacher) for what goes wrong and essentially feels that nothing he does makes a difference. While initially accepting his feelings and checking to make sure his accusations are in fact groundless, the teacher must keep in mind that the youngster habitually sees others rather than himself as the reason things happen to him. Part of the strategy with such a child is to free the teacher from this role in the child's eyes. Again, an interaction with the child should be depersonalized and should refer to the child's own gains and instrumental actions, so that the child does not continue to see the teacher as an all-powerful figure to be resisted or given in to.

A final caution is warranted, particularly when working with children characterized by negative or defiant behavior. If the teacher is upset or angry, it is best to avoid interpersonal interaction for the moment. It is best not to display open anger or loss of control, though it is human to feel such emotions. Knowing beforehand which behaviors might upset a teacher should lead to a plan for handling them when they do occur. Such a plan usually requires a thought-out set of responses including personal discussions at a calm point for both teacher and child.

Once having expressed these cautions, however, it is worth repeating the central point: the personal, one-to-one interaction between child and teacher is a useful and powerful strategy, one that is feasible if used flexibly and irreplaceable when used with appropriate caution. It is not merely a way of being liked, though a teacher who is liked and admired by a student stands a better chance of influencing the youngster to change. The one-to-one contact is often the only or most economical way of getting information, showing interest, expressing a feeling, making a mutual decision, and in general reasserting that the learning setting is an interpersonal enterprise involving more than the input, retention, output and evaluation of facts.

The teacher as a model

Every child enters the classroom with a set of expectations regarding the teacher. The child who always sees adults as determiners of what will happen to him expects the teacher to be arbitrary and all-powerful; the child with angry, negative feelings sees the teacher as judge and jury; the anxious child expects to be pressured and evaluated; the uninvolved child often expects the teacher to be inconsistent and untrustworthy. These expectations derive from prior social relations with adults, including teachers, who have acted these ways, thus causing the child to view them as the source of frustration, failure and hurt. How the child acts depends greatly upon what he has learned to expect from significant adults. By implication, the teacher as model can affect the child's expectations and behavior in both nonproductive and productive ways.

Previous chapters have pointed to how the teacher may function positively as a model in effecting productive change in the child. For the impatient child the teacher can be a model of the reflective person who thinks through a task and talks about pros and cons and possible consequences, before deciding what to do and how to do it. For the intellectually reliant child the teacher can be someone who shows how to make decisions on his own and how to perservere despite obstacles or differing opinions. For the anxious youngster the teacher can be someone who does not get upset because he does not know everything; and for the negative or restless child the teacher can be someone who respects rules, is willing to discuss limits, but who lives up to rules in a non-arbitrary and equitable fashion. Children watch how adults behave and will emulate those actions. An impulsive adult, unwilling to explore ideas and possibilities, dogmatic in approach, who is quick to become upset if contradicted, cannot help the child achieve self-restraint, open-mindedness, and frustration tolerance.

The teacher must remain aware that he is a model, and that to be effective he should plan his strategies with this in mind, maximizing his influence by dramatizing and putting into words what is to be done. This is best accomplished when the teacher clearly spells out in words what he is doing and why he is doing it in this manner, when he encourages the child to do it just like him, and then praises the child for this behavior. Being such a model may seem like a terrible burden to bear, but the fact that the teacher is always a potential model to the child cannot be erased by ignoring it. We would suggest that the best approach is to recognize modeling as a positive force for change and as a tool available to the teacher in achieving his goals.

The positive classroom environment

There is remarkable consistency in all strategies on emphasizing ways of reacting that will create a positive emotional tone in the classroom. This does not mean an absence of tension, of the excitement of novelty, or of emotion. Rather, a wide variety of strategies all tend to create a setting wherein the child can anticipate a positive reaction to what he is doing and a nonjudgmental attitude toward him personally.

Confronted with a variety of problem areas, a common strategy is to encourage, through recognition or praise, the behaviors the teacher desires, the achievements the child reveals, and even at times behaviors that only partially reach these goals. This is done with a smile, a pat on the back or, with certain children, concrete rewards. Such positive reaction must never be unwarranted by the child's actual performance or inconsistent with the child's self-image. The teacher loses credibility when he tells an overreliant child what an independent worker he is. We are all too prone, both as teachers and parents, to take a child's achievements for granted as though they are to be expected, and to focus attention on what the child is not doing right. What we suggest is the opposite orientation: to maximize attention upon desired behavioral goals, and to support their emergence by appropriate recognition.

The goal of accentuating the positive can also be reached by mechanical means, including lights that go on for immediate reward or to inform the child that he is proceeding correctly. Some strategies recommend the use of charts on which the child records his achievements or clocks his work to indicate good performance. These too are part of the total picture since they serve as guides and supports for desirable behavior. They inform the child that he is doing well with an immediacy that might not otherwise be possible for the teacher confronted with a group of children. In combination with more personal teacher (and at times peer) reactions, the classroom becomes a total affirming environment that says: "Yes," "Good," "You're doing fine."

The second quality in creating and maintaining this positive tone is the nonjudgmental attitude of the teacher toward the child as a person. What a child does may be at issue, but never what he "is." No strategy suggests that a child be labeled in a negative fashion. The intellectually reliant child is never told to stop acting "like a baby" or that he is a "cheater." The child who is anxious about performing is not told that he is "silly" to be afraid. The child who feels powerless and thus blames others for everything is not accused of "making excuses." Whatever a child feels just below the surface of his actions must be accepted as a fact and as a part of the child at that moment.

In a variety of situations wherein the teacher may be accused (e.g., "The test was too hard"), the work belittled (e.g., "This English is stupid"), or the teacher called unfair, the first reaction should not be to defend or justify what is criticized. The first reaction is to examine the possible validity of the student's comments and to explore and discuss the dissent in an effort to discover the motives that lie behind the child's feeling. In no strategy is there the suggestion that a child be embarrassed, ridiculed, or frightened for what he does or says. Mild punishments in the form of lost privileges or "soft" reprimands can be useful, but never as a means of personal retaliation on the part of the teacher or as embarrassment of the child in front of the class. When negative consequences must be used, they should always have the purpose of helping the child relate what he does to what follows, in a cause and effect chain. The teacher is not punishing the child for being "bad" but for what he did. A "time out" from activity or from the classroom is preplanned so that the child (and at times the entire class) understands that the purpose is to help the youngster calm down so that he can return. If the child is rebuked, it is a private matter between him and the teacher. If peers are involved in any way, it is made clear that everyone has a role in helping the youngster.

A nonjudgmental attitude is also manifest in the variety of strategies designed to encourage the child to generate and share his ideas and opinions without concern over issues of "right or wrong" or competition with others. The classroom is not only a place to learn facts and specific intellectual skills, important as these are. The classroom is also a place to express and share ideas and feelings, to raise possibilities and explore probabilities, to relate personal experience and feelings to current topics, and to have a dialogue with others in which everyone contributes their unique ideas. Through this nonjudgmental attitude the teacher conveys that an important and valued part of learning is having and sharing experiences.

Clarifying environmental demands

In a number of specific strategies the teacher establishes, often in consort with the child, what it is that is expected of the child. The teacher may let the child know directly what behaviors are acceptable or unacceptable, either in private conversation or through general class discussion: rules of social conduct are spelled out for the negative or restless, disruptive child; "manners" involved in group discussions are clarified for the child who interrupts with irrelevant comments.

A number of strategies involve careful specification of directions and the relationship between what is produced and these directions. The impatient child is focused on directions for a task before proceeding through the task, at times to the point of actually writing the directions out on paper. Directions are kept simple with the overreliant child so that he grasps them and uses them as a guide in his subsequent work. In all of this, the demands implicit in the process of schoolwork are made explicit. Following directions, setting goals, planning action, reviewing one's work all become a focus of instruction in their own right. No assumption is made that the required habits or work skills exist, or that the child will grasp and automatically meet the demands for these skills when given a task.

Other strategies alert or signal the child at crucial times to remind him of something he should or should not do, or to ready him for something that will happen. The inattentive child's name is called out a short time before he is asked a question; another child is signaled that his behavior is becoming unacceptable; an uninvolved child is alerted to the fact that he will be experiencing something during a trip that relates to an element of his classwork; an anxious child is told that he will be asked a question on a topic the next day. In all instances, the teacher is helping the child to predict what is coming and to develop stable expectations about his environment.

Finally, many specific strategies involve timers, lights, clocks, or other mechanical devices that tell the child how he is doing with his work at the moment, how he has been doing, and how close he is to completing it. In this sense, such impersonal signals are actually guides for the child that keep him on the track and cue him when he is slipping.

The common element in all of these teaching strategies is clarification for the child as to exactly where he is and what the environment expects of him. At one point this may involve clarification of directions or how to get started on a task (i.e., where the child is to go and how he is to get there). But clarification is also supplied when there is discussion of rules of conduct and social behavior, and when alerting signposts are used that tell the child how well he is proceeding or that he must get back on the track. While clarification of expectations and demands is very likely necessary in teaching all children, it is especially necessary when working with most behaviorally troubled children. Attention to the end product is not sufficient insofar as it assumes that the child can manage all the prior steps necessary in the process of arriving at an end product. Without the added effort to clarify the process, the child is likely to miss the point of what he must do, break a rule he never appreciated to begin with, and then fail without understanding why.

Fostering self-control
and independent problem-solving

Of all the common elements in the teaching strategies, this one aims most directly at achieving a basic educational as well as mental health goal: individuals who are inner-directed, self-controlled, and intellectually independent. This area is comprised of strategies that (1) foster the generation of thought and expression, (2) involve self-monitoring and self-recording, (3) encourage verbalization of the student's own thoughts and feelings, and (4) involve the student in decision-making.

Strategies that encourage the child to generate and express his own ideas have already been discussed as part of a teacher's nonjudgmental approach in fostering a positively toned environment. They include strategies to encourage explanation of possibilities, the "why" of things and probable outcomes of events, and the free expression of opinions and desires in the classroom independent of the issue of "right or wrong" or whose idea is better. These techniques are aimed at creating more tolerance of unusual personal opinions, an open-minded approach to problems, as well as a respect by the child for his own thoughts, opinions and desires because they are his. Such habitual free exercise of thought, by bringing about greater intellectual self-confidence, ultimately should move the youngster toward sustained and independent achievement. Creating an environment for such loosening up of thinking requires that the teacher foster a social climate of suspended judgment and excitement in ideas.

Self-regulation and independence of mind are also furthered by strategies wherein the child is to record and monitor his own performance. Examples include times when the impatient, unreflective child uses charts or calendars to record and plan his work; the restless, disturbing child keeps a chart to record every time he leaves his seat; or the inattentive child checks off on a card each time he catches his mind wandering from classwork or a discussion. In all instances, the devices are meant to enhance self-critical and self-controlling functioning in which the child himself assesses what he is doing and relates it to the goals he wishes to achieve. Guidance and correction are not coming from outside. The child himself makes the connection between what he has accomplished, his own efforts, and his initial goals.

The third type of strategy designed to foster self-control and independent problem-solving encourages the child to verbalize to himself what he wishes to achieve, what he must do, how he must do it, what he must watch out for, and that he must not rush but instead must persist at a slower pace to solve the problem. This process of "self-instructing," first out loud and in imitation of the teacher, but eventually by himself to himself, establishes a self-guiding way of thinking.

Finally, there are a variety of occasions in which the child is engaged in a decision-making process about his classwork. The reliant child is slowly guided into making simple decisions to the point where he can decide what he wishes to do, out of many possibilities, and how. The anxious child decides what questions should comprise a test he will take, or when he is ready to be called upon to perform in front of others. The child who felt powerless in determining what would happen to him now estimates how much he should do, what time he should allot to it, proceeds with his work, and eventually evaluates his own success and modifies his subsequent expectations. In all of these, the strategy is to get the child to act purposefully on the basis of his own best judgment at the time, and to risk success and failure because he has gained confidence in his ability to make decisions for himself.

The general and the specific

Having highlighted certain common elements in teaching strategies, it is important to emphasize that awareness of these common elements is not sufficient in itself for devising a plan to help a child. After observing and specifying the behaviors that hinder academic achievement and classroom success, there is no substitute for considering the kinds of specific teaching strategies detailed in preceding chapters. The common elements discussed here comprise a teaching approach we would recommend to all teachers. They define a general orientation we judge necessary in working with all behaviorally troubled children. However, when working with a child with a particular difficulty, it is essential that the variety of specific alternative strategies be considered, from which a plan may be devised and implemented to help that child achieve academic success.

References

Foreword

Ringness, T. A. *Mental health in the schools.* New York: Random House, 1968.

Chapter 1

Bower, E. M. *Early identification of emotionally handicapped children in school.* Springfield, Illinois: C. C. Thomas, 1960.

Chazan, M. and Jackson, S. Behavior problems in the infant school. *Journal of Child Psychology and Psychiatry,* 1971, *12,* 191-210.

Deutsch, M. Minority group and class status as related to social and personality factors in scholastic achievement. *Society for Applied Anthropology,* 1960, Monograph 2.

Dreikurs, R., Grunwald, D. B. and Pepper, F. C. *Maintaining sanity in the classroom.* New York: Harper and Row, 1971.

Glavin, J. P. and Quay, H. C. Behavior disorders. *Review of Educational Research,* 1969, *39,* 83-102.

Greenberg, J. W., Gerver, J. M., Challe, J. and Davidson, H. H. Attitudes of children from a deprived environment toward achievement related concepts. *Journal of Educational Psychology,* 1965, *59,* 57-61.

Joint Commission on Mental Health of Children, Inc. *Digest of Crisis In Child Mental Health: Challenge for the 1970's.* Washington, D.C.: Joint Commission on Mental Health of Children, Inc., 1969.

Kellam, S. G. and Schiff, S. K. Adaptation and mental illness in the first grade classrooms of an urban community. *Psychiatric Research Report 21, American Psychiatric Association,* 1968, 79-91.

Pringle, M. L. *11,000 Seven-year-olds: First Report of the National Child Development Study.* London: Longmans, 1966.

Rogers, C. R. Mental health findings in three elementary schools.

Educational Research Bulletin 21, 1942, 69-79.

Silver, A. A. and Hagen, R. A. Profile of a first grade: A basis for preventive psychiatry. *Journal of the American Academy of Child Psychiatry*, 1972, *4*, 645-674.

Spivack, G. and Swift, M. S. Behavioral adjustment in the open classroom. *International Journal of Applied Psychology*, in press.

Spivack, G. and Swift, M. S. The Devereux Elementary School Behavior Rating Scale: A study of the nature and organization of achievement related disturbed classroom behavior. *Journal of Special Education*, 1966, *1*, 71-91.

Stennett, R. G. Emotional handicap in the elementary years: Phase or disease? *American Journal of Orthopsychiatry*, 1966, *36*, 444-449.

Swift, M. S. and Spivack, G. The assessment of achievement related classroom behavior. *Journal of Special Education*, 1968, *2*, 137-153.

Swift, M. S. and Spivack, G. Clarifying the relationship between academic success and overt classroom behavior. *Exceptional Children*, 1969, *36*, 99-104.

Swift, M. S. and Spivack, G. Therapeutic teaching: A review of teaching methods for behaviorally troubled children. *Journal of Special Education*, 1974, in press.

Swift, M. S., Spivack, G., Danset, A., Danset-Léger, J. and Winnykamen, F. Classroom behavior and academic success of French and American elementary schoolchildren. *International Review of Applied Psychology*, 1, *21*, 1972.

Ullmann, C. A. *Identification of maladjusted school children.* Public Health Monograph, 7, 1957.

United States Department of Health, Education and Welfare, Public Health Service. *Behavior patterns of children in school. Vital Health Statistics* (Roberts, J. and Baird, J., Jr.), 1972.

Wall, W. D. *Education and mental health.* Paris: UNESCO, 1955.

Wall, W. D. (Ed.). *Psychological services for schools.* New York: University Press, 1956.

Chapter 2

Austin, M. C., Bush, C. L. and Huebner, M. H. *Reading evaluation.* New York: Ronald Press Co., 1961.

Borton, T. *Reach, touch and teach: Student concerns and process education.* New York: McGraw-Hill, 1970.

Broden, M., Hall, R. V. and Mitts, B. The effect of self-recording on the classroom behavior of two eighth-grade students. *Journal of Applied Behavior Analysis,* 1971, *4,* 191-199.

Bruner, J. S. *Toward a theory of instruction.* Cambridge, Massachusetts: Harvard University Press, 1966.

Cruickshank, W. M., Junkala, J. B. and Paul, J. L. *The preparation of teachers of brain-injured children.* Syracuse: Syracuse University Press, 1968.

Gregory, T. B. *Encounters with teaching: A micro-teaching manual.* Englewood Cliffs, New Jersey: Prentice-Hall, 1972.

Hall, R. V., Lund, P. and Jackson, P. Effects of teacher attention on study behavior. *Journal of Applied Behavior Analysis,* 1968, *1,* 1-12.

Kounin, J. S. An analysis of teachers' managerial techniques. *Psychology in the Schools,* 1967, *4,* 221-227.

Kounin, J. S. and Obradovic, S. Managing emotionally disturbed children in regular classrooms: A replication and extension. *Journal of Special Education,* 1968, *2,* 129-136.

Kroth, R. Behavior management techniques. Paper presented at the Council for Exceptional Children, 46th International Conference, March 1968.

Lovitt, T. C. and Smith, J. O. Effects of instructions on an individual's verbal behavior. *Exceptional Children,* 1972, *38,* 685-693.

Quay, H. C., Werry, J. S., McQueen, M. and Sprague, R. L. Remediation of the conduct problem child in the special class setting. *Exceptional Children,* 1966, *32,* 509-515.

Willis, J. and Crowder, J. A portable device for group modification of classroom attending behavior. *Journal of Applied Behavior Analysis,* 1972, *5,* 199-202.

Chapter 3

Lovitt, T. C. Self-management projects with children with behavioral difficulties. *Journal of Learning Disabilities*, 1973, *6*, 138-150.

Spivack, G. and Shure, M. *Social adjustment of young children: A cognitive approach to solving real-life problems.* San Francisco: Jossey-Bass, 1973.

Tribble, A. and Hall, R. V. Effects of peer approval on completion of arithmetic assignments. In F. W. Clark, D. R. Evans and L. A. Hamerlynck (Eds.), *Implementing behavioral programs for schools and clinics: The proceedings of the Third Banff International Conference on Behavior Modification.* Champaign, Illinois: Research Press Co., 1972, 139-140.

Chapter 4

Becker, W. C., Madsen, C. H., Arnold, C. R. and Thomas, B. A. The contingent use of teacher attention and praise in reducing classroom behavior problems. *Journal of Special Education*, 1967, *1*, 287-307.

Borton, T. *Reach, touch and teach: Student concerns and process education.* New York: McGraw-Hill, 1970.

Bruner, J. S. *Toward a theory of instruction.* Cambridge, Massachusetts: Harvard University Press, 1966.

Buys, C. J. Effects of teacher reinforcement on elementary pupils' behavior and attitudes. *Psychology in the Schools*, 1972, *9*, 278-288.

Engelhardt, L., Sulzer, B. and Altekruse, M. The counselor as a consultant in eliminating out-of-seat behavior. *Elementary School Guidance and Counseling*, 1971, *5*, 196-204.

Frymier, J. R. A study of students' motivation to do good work in school. *Journal of Educational Research*, 1964, *57*, 239-244.

Schwebel, A. I. and Cherlin, D. L. Physical and social distancing in teacher-pupil relationship. *Journal of Educational Psychology*, 1972, *63*, 543-550.

Spivack, G. Behavioral traits that characterize "admired" and "not admired" staff in a residential treatment center, as viewed by male adolescent students. Unpublished manuscript, 1965.

Whitley, A. D. and Sulzer, B. Reducing disruptive behavior through consultation. *Personnel and Guidance Journal*, 1970, *48*, 836-841.

Chapter 5

Kagan, J., Pearson, L. and Welch, L. Conceptual impulsivity and inductive reasoning. *Child Development*, 1966, *37*, 359-365.

Kagan. J. Reflection-impulsivity and reading ability in primary grade children. *Child Development*, 1965, *36*, 609-628.

Kagan, J. Reflection-impulsivity: The generality and dynamics of conceptual tempo. *Journal of Abnormal Psychology*, 1966, *71*, 17-24.

Meichenbaum, D. H. and Goodman, J. Training impulsive children to talk to themselves: A means of developing self-control. *Journal of Abnormal Psychology*, 1971, *77*, 115-126.

Spivack, G. and Shure, M. *Social adjustment of young children: A cognitive approach to solving real-life problems.* San Francisco: Jossey-Bass, 1974.

Yando, R. M. and Kagan, J. The effect of teacher tempo on the child. *Child Development*, 1968, *39*, 27-34.

Chapter 6

Erikson, E. *Childhood and society.* New York: W. W. Norton and Co., 1963.

Friedman, P. Relationship of teacher reinforcement to spontaneous student verbalization within the classroom. *Journal of Educational Psychology*, 1973, *65*, 59-64.

Mussen, P. and Kuhlman, C. Initiating responses. In J. Bruner (Ed.), *Learning about learning.* USDHEW Cooperative Research Monograph No. 15, 1966, 14-21.

Shure, M. B. and Spivack, G. Means-ends thinking, adjustment and social class among elementary-school-aged children. *Journal of Consulting and Clinical Psychology*, 1972, *38*, 348-353.

Spivack, G. and Shure, M. B. *Social adjustment of young children: A cognitive approach to solving real-life problems.* San Francisco: Jossey-Bass, 1974.

Swift, M. S. Training poverty mothers in communication skills. *The Reading Teacher,* 1970, *23,* 360-367.

Torrance, E. P. and Myers, R. E. *Creative learning and teaching.* New York: Dodd, Mead and Co., 1971.

Torrance, E. P. and Torrance, P. Combining creative problem-solving with creative expression activities in the education of disadvantaged young people. *The Journal of Creative Behavior,* 1972, *6,* 1-10.

Chapter 7

Dreikurs, R., Grunwald, D. B. and Pepper, F. C. *Maintaining sanity in the classroom.* New York: Harper and Row, 1971.

Henle, M. Cognitive skills. In J. Bruner (Ed.), *Learning about learning.* USDHEW Cooperative Research Monograph No. 15, 1966.

Kagan, J., Pearson, L. and Welch, L. Modifiability of an impulsive tempo. *Journal of Educational Psychology,* 1966, *57,* 359-365.

Redl, R. and Wineman, D. *Controls from within.* Glencoe: The Free Press, 1952.

Spivack, G. and Shure, M. *Social adjustment of young children: A cognitive approach to solving real-life problems.* San Francisco: Jossey-Bass, 1974.

Spivack, G. and Swift, M. Behavioral adjustment in the open classroom. *International Journal of Applied Psychology,* in press.

Chapter 8

Barrish, H. H., Saunders, M. and Wolf, M. M. Good behavior game: Effects of individual contingencies for group consequences on disruptive behavior in a classroom. *Journal of Applied Behavior Analysis,* 1969, *2,* 119-124.

Gallagher, P. A. Structuring academic tasks for emotionally disturbed boys. *Exceptional Children,* 1972, *38,* 711-720.

Giebink, J. W., Stover, D. O. and Fahl, M. A. Teaching adaptive responses to frustration to emotionally disturbed boys. *Journal of Consulting and Clinical Psychology*, 1968, *32*, 366-368.

Gnagey, W. J., Goodwin, P. L., Jabker, E. H., Shaw, K. B. and McCormick, M. P. The use of group and individual rewards to reduce deviance in a high school classroom. Unpublished manuscript, 1971.

Haring, N. and Phillips, E. *Educating emotionally disturbed children.* New York: McGraw-Hill, 1962.

Kubany, E. S., Weiss, L. E. and Sloggett, B. B. The good behavior clock: A reinforcement time out procedure for reducing disruptive behavior. *Journal of Behavior Therapy and Experimental Psychiatry*, 1971, *2*, 173-179.

Long, N. J. and Newman, R. G. A differential approach to the management of surface behavior of children in school. *Bulletin of the School of Education of Indiana University*, 1961, *37*, 47-61.

Newman, R. G. The acting out boy. *Exceptional Children*, 1956, *22*, 186-190, 204-216.

Newman, R. G. The assessment of progress in the treatment of hyper-aggressive children with learning disturbances within a school setting. *American Journal of Orthopsychiatry*, 1959, *29*, 633-643.

Ramp, E., Ulrich, R. and Dulaney, S. Delayed time out as a procedure for reducing disruptive classroom behavior: A case study. *Journal of Applied Behavior Analysis*, 1971, *4*, 235-239.

Redl, F. and Wineman, D. *Controls from within.* Glencoe: The Free Press, 1952.

Sarason, S. B., Levine, M., Goldenberg, I. I., Cherlin, D. L. and Bennett, E. M. *Psychology in community settings.* New York: John Wiley and Sons, 1966.

Wasik, B. H., Senn, K., Welch, R. H. and Cooper, B. R. Behavior modification with culturally deprived school children: Two case studies. *Journal of Applied Behavior Analysis*, 1969, *2*, 181-194.

Whelan, R. F. and Haring, N. G. Modification in maintenance of behavior through systematic application of consequences. Paper presented at 43rd Annual Convention of the Council for Exceptional Children, 1965.

215

Chapter 9

Bruner, J. S. *Toward a theory of instruction.* Cambridge, Massachusetts: Harvard University Press, 1966.

Dreikurs, R., Grunwald, D. B. and Pepper, F. C. *Maintaining sanity in the classroom.* New York: Harper and Row, 1971.

Gaudry, E. and Spielberger, C. D. *Anxiety and educational achievement.* New York: John Wiley and Sons, 1971.

Mussen, P. and Kuhlman, C. D. Initiating responses. In J. Bruner (Ed.), *Learning about learning.* USDHEW Cooperative Research Monograph No. 15, 1966, 14-27.

Sarason, S. B., Davidson, K. S., Lighthall, F. F., Waite, R. and Ruebush, B. *Anxiety in elementary school children.* New York: John Wiley and Sons, 1960.

Chapter 10

Blackwood, R. O. The operant conditioning of verbally mediated self-control in the classroom. *Journal of School Psychology,* 1970, *8,* 251-258.

Bower, E. M. *Early identification of emotionally handicapped children in school.* Springfield, Illinois: C. C. Thomas, 1969.

Broden, M., Bruce, C., Mitchell, M. A., Carter, V. and Hall, R. V. Effects of teacher attention on attending behavior of two boys of adjacent desks. *Journal of Applied Behavior Analysis,* 1971, *4,* 191-199.

Dickinson, D. J. Changing behavior with behavioral techniques. *Journal of School Psychology,* 1968, *6,* 278-283.

Hall, R. V., Axelrod, S., Foundopoulos, M., Shellman, J., Campbell, R. A. and Cranston, S. S. The effective use of punishment to modify behavior in the classroom. In O'Leary, K. D. and O'Leary, S. G. (Eds.), *Classroom management: The successful use of behavior modification.* New York: Pergamon Press, Inc., 1972, pp. 173-182.

Hall, R. V., Lund, D. and Jackson, D. Effects of teacher attention on study behavior. *Journal of Applied Behavior Analysis,* 1968, *1,* 1-12.

Homme, L. et al. *How to use contingency contracting in the classroom.* Champaign, Illinois: Research Press Co., 1970.

Kounin, J. S. and Obradovic, S. Managing emotionally disturbed children in regular classrooms: A replication and extension. *The Journal of Special Education,* 1968, *2,* 129-135.

Kroth, R. Behavior management techniques. Paper presented at Council for Exceptional Children, 46th International Conference, New York, 1968.

McClain, W. A. The modification of aggressive classroom behavior through reinforcement, inhibition, and relationship therapy. *Training School Bulletin,* 1969, *65,* 122-125.

O'Leary, K. D., Kaufman, K. F., Kass, R. E. and Drabman, R. S. The effects of loud and soft reprimands on the behavior of disruptive students. *Exceptional Children,* 1970, *37,* 145-155.

Redl, F. and Wineman, D. *Controls from within.* Glencoe: The Free Press, 1952.

Redl, F. The concept of punishment. In Long, N. J., Morse, W. C. and Newman, R. G. (Eds.), *Conflict in the classroom.* Belmont, California: Wadsworth Publishing Company, Inc., 1965.

Solomon, R. W. and Wahler, R. G. Peer reinforcement control of classroom problem behavior. *Journal of Applied Behavior Analysis,* 1973, *6,* 49-56.

Spivack, G. and Swift, M. Behavioral Adjustment in the open classroom. *International Journal of Applied Psychology,* in press.